CLASS STRUGGLES
IN ZAMBIA
1889–1989

THE FALL OF
KENNETH KAUNDA
1990–1991

MUNYONZWE HAMALENGWA
B.A.; M.A., LL.B., Ph.D (1992)

Barrister & Solicitor
602–175 Shaughnessy Blvd.
Willowdale, Ontario
Canada M2J 1K1
(416) 496–9549

UNIVERSITY
PRESS OF
AMERICA

Lanham • New York • London

Library of Congress Cataloging-in-Publication Data

Hamalengwa, M.
Class struggles in Zambia, 1889–1989, and the fall of Kenneth Kaunda,
1990–1991 / Munyonzwe Hamalengwa.
p.   cm.
Includes bibliographical references and index.
1. Working class—Zambia—Political activity—History.
2. Industrial relations—Zambia—History.   3. Democracy—
Zambia—History.   4. Zambia—Politics and government.   I. Title.
HD8803.H36   1992   305.5'096894—dc20   92–14695 CIP

ISBN 0–8191–8741–0 (cloth : alk. paper)

For my daughter Kubota Hamalengwa,

Thanks for the happiness and sunshine
you have brought me.

Acknowledgements

This is an attempt at an outline of class struggles in Zambia between 1889 – 1989. The working class in pre-independence and post-independence Zambia has performed an exemplary role in the struggle for social liberation for the working class as well as the general population. Their history deserves to be told as fully as research materials allow. Herein I document and fill in some of the gaps about working class struggles that have been prevalent, particularly in the post-independence era.

The premise of this study is that the maintenance of fragile democracy in Zambia has been dependent on the existence of a strong and autonomous labour movement. As the struggles for genuine democracy in the developing countries intensify, the role of the working classes will increasingly become pivotal. This study is aimed at documenting the role the Zambian working class has performed and is likely to perform in the struggle for democracy in Zambia.

I have conducted research for this study in Zambia, London, Geneva, Toronto, Ottawa, Washington, D.C., as well as Cambridge and York Universities. In some of these places I have been fortunate enough to be assisted by able librarians whom I would like to thank for their assistance. Even if I do not name them, I will forever be grateful.

Two friends read the entire draft and made very useful suggestions some of which I have incorporated. Thanks must be recorded to Dickson Eyoh and Derrick Chitala for their time and critical comments, in this regard.

My family in Zambia: my Father, Timothy Hamalengwa; Mother, Josephine Namoonga; my Brothers, Mwanga and Listene Hamalengwa; and my Sister, Angelinah Hamalengwa have supplied undying motivation all these years despite the distance. What more can I say: I love you and thanks ever so much. But I apologize for abandoning you. I know you understand the reason for my absence.

Many friends have also been in touch and have assisted in numerous ways towards the completion of this study: I wish to acknowledge my comradeship with Phillip Chilomo, Samuel Miyanda, Dr. Mary Miyanda, Dr. Jotham Moomba, Dr. Ackson Kanduza, the late Afro Himwiinga, Dr. Julius Ihonvbere, Dr. Ademuni Odeke, Dr. Daudi Mukangara, Dave Moore and so many others too numerous to name. Another day.

I thank my typist and typesetter, Linda Radomski, for speedy and reliable work in getting this manuscript out.

My wife Lucy endured long absences and the accompanying agonies. So much to thank you for my dear. My Daughter Kubota, this one is for you.

To the Zambian working class, this is my contribution to the common heritage of Zambia.

Munyonzwe Hamalengwa
February 1991
Toronto, Canada

Contents

1

Introduction:
The Struggle Between Labour and Capital

The ruling class in Zambia has since independence in 1964 tried to incorporate the labour movement as a subordinate and subservient social entity by various methods, either peacefully or forcefully. Some of these have included; (1) an attempt to take over the Mineworkers Union of Zambia (MUZ) leadership in 1966, (2) an attempt to remove trade union organization in a one-party state, (3) vetting of trade union leaders aspiring for office in a trade union by the party, (4) an attempt to transform the Zambia Congress of Trade Unions (ZCTU) into a wing of the party, (5) repression by arresting and detaining labour leaders, and (6) by introduction of a labour code, etc. By declaring most workers as essential workers and forbidden to strike, the right to strike has been forbidden by decree. These efforts have been resisted by the labour movement. In a country which had a one-party state, where all autonomous organizations such as political parties, student organizations and so on had been suppressed and banished, the relative success of the labour movement to maintain an independent existence has been quite impressive.

Most of the studies on the post colonial societies have been limited to the analysis of the state and the various ruling groups vying for state control. The other social forces i.e. working classes, peasantry, petty bourgeoisie etc. have largely been ignored. Where they have been taken note of, for example, the working class, most studies have tried to fit these social forces in pre-conceived categories, either as labour aristocracies or how they can be politicised in order to fulfil their "revolutionary" role. These social forces have not been analyzed in terms of their own inherent limitations or capacities and their relationships to ruling groups over a long period of time.

This study limits itself to the study of the interaction between the ruling groups in Zambia and the working classes organised in the ZCTU. This study, using Jeff Crisp's framework of *Labour control* and *Labour resistance* tries to show: (1) that instead of focusing attention on the state and ruling groups at the exclusion of other social forces, particularly the working class etc., we must shift our attention to include the labour movement and its interaction with the ruling groups. This I believe helps us to understand, deeper, the dynamics of the political process in the post colonial era, (2) That contrary to the assertions that the Zambian labour movement has been incorporated as a labour aristocracy, this study will show that the Zambian labour movement has been politically dynamic within the limitations permitted by the repressive One-Party State system in Zambia. It has been somewhat of a countervailing force to the omnipresent and perversive existence of the party and its government, (3) That instead of seeing the Zambian labour movement as a labour aristocracy and constituting a right wing opposition to an otherwise progressive socialist government, this study will try to demonstrate that the behaviour of the labour movement has been part and parcel of class struggle against a ruling class that has been bent on appropriating more and more surplus for itself, (4) That in the process of class struggle, the Zambian working class wrung for itself a "democratic space" which was increasingly although grudgingly recognised and respected by the ruling class as well as fully accepted by the majority of the people. This democratic space could be very crucial in the future political and economic developments in the country.

Though a tired argument by now, I will start by discussing the characterization of the working class as a labour aristocracy and then move on to dismantle this characterization as it relates to the Zambian working class.

The Labour Aristocracy Thesis

The roots of this thesis goes back to classical Marxism. Frantz Fanon seems to have opened the way in Africa in regarding the working class there as the corrupted and pampered ally of the indigenous bourgeoisie. They are "the most comfortably off fraction of the people" and they still want "more" loot even if they fear that their demands would "scandalize the rest of the nation". The same argument that would be used by African ruling classes to control working class organizations! The labour aristocracy is a mixed lot indeed, for according to Govan Arrighi it includes the "elite", "sub-elite" and the "proletariat proper".[2] The labour aristocracy thesis is premised on the supposed "numerous and generous benefits enjoyed by workers – high wages, good conditions of work, housing, the use of complex and modern technology and therefore the concentration of trained manpower in the industry. The literature also emphasizes the integration of the workers into the capitalist system through the domestication and incorporation of [their] unions". According to Julius Ihonvbere, "an almost teleological version of this position presents ... workers as 'helpless' workers who have no control over their actions; these are shaped by technology and the high salaries provided by the companies. However, little theoretical or empirical evidence is usually provided to justify the description of workers as 'labour aristocrats'".[3] Because of their structural location and privileges, these labour aristocracies "identify upwards" and that their organizations play a self-interested and conservative role.[4] However, according to Richard Sandbrook:

> To constitute a labour aristocracy, a group of organized workers must not only be relatively privileged, but also perceive itself as having interests separate from, and indeed opposed to, those of the lower strata or classes. One cannot infer that such a perception exists merely on the grounds of an income differential and the presence of a large "industrial reserve army" in the towns. Although the situation will vary from place to place, there are certain widely operating social and economic factors tending to associate urban workers with popular interests and grievances to make them men of the people.[5]

To demonstrate the above, requires empirical research, which the proponents of the labour aristocracy thesis have simply not generally undertaken. Theirs is based on broad theoretical generalizations of the superficially observable tendencies. This is however not to deny that there are indeed privileged elements within the labour movements and who identify upwards, just as it would not be denied that there are members of the ruling classes who identify downwards. The picture is much more complex than one's location in the division of labour. Empirically there are now some studies which disprove the labour aristocracy thesis.[6] There are also some studies which do not deny the existence of what appears to be a labour aristocracy or what they prefer to describe as 'privileged' and 'conservative' elements amongst the organized working class in Africa.[7] Drawing on empirical data however, they have been able to demonstrate that the economic, social and political arguments often advanced by the labour aristocracy theorists had no basis.[8]

The critics of the labour aristocracy thesis have shown through empirical research that the emphasis on life styles, higher wages, residence and aspirations of the "aristocracy" do not bear out the positions of the advocates. These critics have shown that the higher cost of living in the urban centres and the remittances by urban workers to rural relatives all operate as a check on the rise of the absolute wage level.[9] Piet Konings' study of Valco workers at Tema in fact demonstrated among other things that the workers identified "downwards" with the "suffering" social groups of Ghanaian society among whom they lived and maintained close social and economic ties.[10] The criticism of the labour aristocracy thesis can be summarized by emphasizing the crucial points thus: (a) the inclusion of all the African working class in the labour aristocracy *a' la* Fanon or lumping together of elites, sub-elites (these comprise of teachers, skilled artisans, executive and clerical grades, top civil servants, managers, personnel in public relations, lawyers and doctors) and "the proletariat proper" as belonging to the labour aristocracy *a' la* Arrighi is simply stretching the analysis too far:[11] (b) equating higher salaries with collaboration or propensity to collaborate with the African ruling classes or with lack of revolutionary credentials is devoid of empirical-historical or theoretical foundation;[12] (c) The point that the working class lives a better life compared to the peasantry has also been criticized, it simply may not be in accord with reality;[13] and (d) equating peasant poverty with propensity to revolutionary consciousness and activity is also without empirical basis in colonial and post-colonial Africa to date.[14]

There has of course been some cautious rethinking on the whole question of the revolutionary credentials or lack of it of the African working class and the concept of labour aristocracy itself.[15]

The questions I will be implicitly answering in this study among others are: To what extent has there been collaboration between the bureaucratic bourgeoisie and the working class in Zambia? To what extent can these be said to constitute an allied labour aristocracy? Has the so-called 'public interest' been demonstrated and what has been done to realize it?

Working Class Struggles

Moving away from the labour aristocracy thesis to working class struggles, we find some shortcomings in the characterization and emphasis in the study of these struggles.

"Studies of African labour issues have been confined to the more overt forms of protest – predominantly strikes, the struggle to unionize and to direct political activity",[16] while "covert" forms of protest have been ignored. One reason why this has been the case is precisely because these overt forms of struggle are the "high water marks of protest",[17] they are eruptions which temporarily give notice of the temperature in the relations between labour and capital or labour and state as the case may be. They may in fact alter the power relations temporarily or permanently in favour or against any of these entities. Otherwise covert forms of protest being latent are not seen to be contributory to the alteration of power relations. In fact this may be false given that it may be through the process of "osmosis" of all these covert forms that result in an eruption. These covert forms may lead to organization by constantly raising the temperature in the work place. Overt and covert forms of struggle thus should be seen as dialectical unities and not as separate events. Referring to the covert forms of protest in Rhodesian mines, Charles Van Onselen says and I wholly agree with him, "At least as important [as overt forms of struggle], if not more so, were the less dramatic, silent and often unorganized responses, and it is this latter set of responses, which occurred on a day-to-day basis that reveal most about the functioning of the system and formed the woof and warp of worker consciousness. Likewise it was the unarticulated, unorganized protest and resistance which the employers and the state found most difficult to detect or suppress".[18]

While this study deals with state control and overt forms of working class struggle in Zambia, i.e. strikes, the above message is relevant to note as it shows that much as the state may pass legislation, declare states of emergency, impose a one-party state system, ban strikes etc., labour uses many forms of resistance some of which may go undetected by the state or employers. This may in fact as Van Onselen says, constitute working class consciousness.

Some of the covert forms of struggles include: desertion; sabotage; deliberate accidents and sickness; drug use; theft; etc. The accumulation of these unheralded forms of protest can in fact reduce however minuscule the profit margins of the political class or private capital. And their use may materially or psychologically satisfy individual workers or segments of workers. This would be a very useful area of research.

Covert but especially overt forms of struggle are for the immediate gains of the working class. This has irked those who would rather have the workers abandon their "trade union consciousness" and "economism" and campaign for long term goals i.e. revolutionary overthrow of capitalist ruling classes. If the workers do not transform themselves from a "class-in-itself" into a "class-for-itself", then those workers are not revolutionary, they are seen to be aligned with the ruling classes. This perspective is far off the mark and I wholly agree with Robin Cohen when he states: "The danger of such a perspective is that it tends to romanticize the proletariat and seek explanations for its frequent failure to live up to its ascribed status as 'the truly revolutionary class' not by looking at its own organizational weakness and ideological limitations but by finding other agencies which systematically are pulling the wool over the proletariat's eyes".[19] Further this perspective fails to note that whether or not the workers are struggling for immediate gains without revolutionary implication, it is still class struggle, it still impacts on power relations between the capitalist class and the working class. The dynamism or otherwise of society has to be located within these class struggles. And it may be due to these class struggles, whether "silent" or "loud" that may open possibilities for change, reform or transformation.

Other studies have already moved in the direction suggested above, vis-a-vis the working class. These studies focus less on structural class position than on worker values and practice and emphasize the process whereby persons involved in wage labour become "a group groping for self-expression and the creation of a corporate identity". In agreement with E. P. Thompson,[20] workers are seen as active agents in the creation of their own group solidarity, consciousness and action. These studies[21] see class as "a happening expressed in shared values, feelings, interests, life experiences, and set in concrete historical events and processes". According to Jane Parpart, they emphasize the special factors affecting class formation and class consciousness, without assuming a linear progression towards a preordained form of consciousness. Looked in this way, worker consciousness and organization are altered by the mode of production and mediated by the slow and partial character of African proletarianization, racial and ethnic divisions, and the nature of class struggle at a particular historic conjuncture.[22] Further, looked at this way may help us understand why working class organizations respond differently in different circumstances: repression may induce mere economism, reformism, populism or revolutionary consciousness etc.

One particular study that has combined the analysis of the state, capital and the working class both during the colonial and the post-colonial times and whose framework this study will adopt is that of Jeff Crisp's, *The Story of an African Working Class.*[23] Crisp sets out the framework through which class struggle was waged by adopting the concepts of Labour control used by the state and capital and Labour resistance used by the working class. *Labour control* is used to denote those activities of the representatives, allies and collaborators of capital which are designed to assert authority over wage labour and thereby incorporate it into the capitalist mode of production. Labour resistance is used to denote those activities of wage labour, its representatives and allies, which defy the authority of capital, assert the autonomy of the worker, and thereby obstruct the incorporation of labour into the capitalist mode of production. Labour control and labour resistance are seen to be integral and inseparable features of the capitalist mode of production. Labour resistance and labour control are a necessary manifestation of capital's principal objective, the accumulation of the surplus value created by labour power. Thus class struggle is a result of capital's desire for accumulation and labour's desire to appropriate more of what it creates. According to Crisp, capital's principal objective of accumulating surplus value is threatened by the resistance of workers. The state, an administrative and juridical structure, relatively autonomous of capital, tries to minimize the impact of such resistance on the rate at which surplus value is created and appropriated.[24]

Capital uses three methods of appropriating surplus. Firstly, it must be able to purchase as much (or as little) labour power as it requires at any time, and bring it into connection with the means of production. It must, therefore, control the *supply* of labour to, and its occupational and geographical distribution within, the wage labour market. Secondly, to maximize the surplus value which it appropriates from labour, capital must control, and thereby minimize the wages paid to the worker, and habituate the worker to the unequal distribution of the product of their labour. Thirdly, capital can also maximize the surplus value appropriated from labour by controlling and thereby maximizing, the *productivity* of the worker, and by habituating the worker to the unequal distribution of effort and authority in the work place.[25]

Further according to Crisp, in order to control the supply, wages, productivity and political activity of labour, capital and the state employ a variety of labour control strategies. Firstly he classifies methods of labour control according to which of the four forms of capitalist control they are designed to reinforce. Taxation, as an example, has commonly been used as a means of forcing rural populations off the land and into the labour market and is therefore used to control the supply of labour. Supervision, on the other hand, is used to control the work-rate or productivity of labour. Then there are other types of labour control: promotion, bonus schemes, deductions from wages etc. as well as paternalism, lock-out etc. are used to control individual workers and collectivities respectively. The state does also use a variety of strategies to control labour: legislative measures to obstruct the unionization of workers, to restrict the financial and administrative autonomy of established unions and to prevent workers from leaving weak trade unions to join or create a more militant organization. The state does also use ideology, e.g. of 'national interest' to divert workers' attention away from the inequalities of capitalist society, and to persuade trade union members and officials to increase output, forgo wage increases and avoid disruptive political activities.[26]

According to Crisp workers also employ a broad spectrum of modes of resistance: (1) 'informal resistance' which includes: absenteeism, sabotage, malingering, theft, desertion etc.; (2) 'collective resistance' which includes: strike, riot, rally, demonstration, go-slow/work to rule etc. and (3) 'institutional resistance' which includes: party formation/membership, pressure group formation/membership, trade union formation/membership.[27]

This study will adopt the framework of labour control and labour resistance as aspects of class struggle as it has been expressed in colonial and post-colonial Zambia, with much emphasis on the latter. Methodologically this study is guided by a three-fold perspective:[28]

1. To shift emphasis from a concentration on objective processes to the subjective factor in Zambian development, not so as to ignore the

objective context of this development but to see it as an ongoing historical outcome of class and social struggles;

2. To shift the focus from the state to the organized working class in Zambia as the subject of history;

3. To shift attention from an abstract search for millennial social movements to a concrete analysis of actual class struggles, historical and contemporary in order to underline their contradictory character.

Notes

1.   Frantz Fanon, *The Wretched of the Earth*, (New York: Grove Press Inc., 1966).

2.   Govan Arrighi, "International Corporations, Labour Aristocracies and Economic Development in Tropical Africa" Arrighi and Saul, *Essays on the Political Economy of Africa*, (New York: Monthly Review Press, 1973).

3.   Julius O. Ihonvbere, *Labour, Transnational Corporations and the State in Nigeria's Oil Industry*, Ph.D. Thesis, University of Toronto, 1984, p. 153.

4.   Ibid.

5.   Richard Sandbrook, "The Political Potential of African Urban Workers", *Canadian Journal of African Studies* XI (3), (1977), p. 421.

6.   Richard Jeffries, *Class, Power and Ideology in Ghana: The Railwaymen of Ghana* (Cambridge: Cambridge University Press, 1978); Piet Konings, "Political Consciousness and Political Action of Industrial Workers in Ghana: A Case of Valco Workers at Tema", *African Perspectives*, (2), (1978) and Keith Hincliffe, "The Kaduna Textile Workers: Characteristics of an African Industrial Labour Force", *Savana II*, (1), (1973).

7.   Ihonvbere, note 3.

8.   See Christopher Allen, "Unions, Incomes and Development", in *Development Trends in Kenya*, (Centre for African Studies: University of Edinburgh, 1972); and Richard Jeffries, "The Labour Aristocracy? A Ghana Case Study", *Review of African Political Economy*, (3), (1977).

9.   Ihonvbere, note 3 p. 156.

10.   Konings, note 6, p. 74., Ihonvbere Ibid.

11.   Jack Woddis, *New Theories of Revolution*, (New York: International Publishers, 1972) ch. 2.

12.   Adrian Peace, "The Lagos Proletariat: Labour Aristocrats or Populist Militants" in *The Development of An African Working Class* edited by Richard Sandbrook and Robin Cohen, (London: Longman, 1975) and Richard Jeffries, note 8.

13.   Woddis, note 11, Samir Amin, "Income Distribution and the 'Privileged' Worker" in *African Social Studies: A Radical Reader* edited by Peter Gutkind and Peter Waterman, (New York: Monthly Review Press, 1977).

14.   Amilcar Cabral, *Revolution in Guinea*, (New York and London: Monthly Review Press, 1969) and Wooddis, note 11.

19.   John Saul, "The Labour Aristocracy Thesis Reconsidered" in Sandbrook and Cohen, note 12.

16.   Robin Cohen, "Resistance and Hidden Forms of Consciousness among African Workers" in *Third World Lives of Struggle* edited by Hazel Johnson and Henry Bernstein, (London: Heinemann, 1982) p. 245.

17. Charles Van Onselen, *Chibaro: African Mine Labour in Southern Rhodesia 1900-1933*, (London: Pluto Press, 1976) p. 227.

18. Ibid.

19. Cohen, note 16, p. 256.

20. E. P. Thompson, *The Making of the English Working Class* (Harmondsworth: Penguin, 1963).

21. See Adrian Peace, "Industrial Protest in Nigeria" in Emanuel de Kadt and Gavin Williams, eds. *Sociology and Development* (London, 1974); Robin Cohen, "From Peasants to Workers in Africa" in Peter C. W. Gutkind and I. Wallerstein, eds. *The Political Economy of Contemporary Africa* (London: Sage, 1976), Jeff Crisp, *The Story of an African Working Class* (London: Zed Press, 1984) among others.

22. Jane Parpart, *Labour and Capital on the African Copperbelt*, (Philadelphia: Temple University Press, 1984) p.11.

23. Note 21.

24. Ibid., pp. 1-3.

25. Ibid., p. 2.

26. Ibid., pp. 3-5.

27. Ibid., p. 6.

28. Adapted from Mamdani et al., "Social Movements, Social Transformation, Democracy and Development in Africa" *CODERSIA Bulletin* Vol. Vlll, No. 2, 1987, pp. 7-ll.

2

Studies on the Zambian Working Class

The labelling of the Zambian working class, particularly the mineworkers, as a labour aristocracy is just one of the weaknesses prevalent in Zambian labour studies. I will deal with this complex issue later. The over-concentration of labour studies on the mineworkers alone is one of the other ones. Virtually all major studies that include books, monographs and articles on the Zambian working class deal with the mineworkers. The best known works are those of Berger; Parpart; Burawoy; Bates etc. While it is easy to understand why the copper mines and mineworkers have received the bulk of the attention – copper and the copper mineworkers have been central to Zambia's economic and political development from the 1920s to the present, this over-concentration has tended to obscure the important role played by the rest of the Zambian working class. In the post-colonial situation it is folly to neglect the contribution of the Zambia Congress of Trade Unions (ZCTU), Zambia National Union of Teachers (ZNUT) the Railway Workers Union of Zambia (RWUZ) and others in Zambia's labour struggles. Some of the unions also played a very important role in economic and political struggles of the 1950s and early 60s.

While this study still reflects the bias towards the coppermines and the copper mineworkers dictated by the central and crucial role played by that industry and workers in it, it tries as much as possible to include the whole Zambian labour movement represented by ZCTU. I try as much as possible to shift the attention to ZCTU as the representative of the working class in Zambia. A lot of work still needs to be done on the political contribution of each union organized in ZCTU. Most of the unions have not been studied fully in their own right. One important factor necessitating the study of ZCTU is that its leadership has borne the brunt of attack by the ruling party in Zambia and the ongoing relationship between the two have been crucial to Zambia's political development.

The most important recent work that has broken out of the over-concentration of the copper industry and copper mineworkers is that of Henry Meebelo, *African Proletarians and Colonial Capitalism: The Origins, Growth and Struggles of the Zambian Labour Movement to 1964*.[1] Not only does this work trace in detail the impetus to the growth of the labour movement as a whole as well as individual unions and the struggles they fought, it is also theoretically well grounded. It weaves radical theories of the working class into the history of the Zambian working class to show the limits as well as possibilities presented by working class struggles in the concrete situation of colonial Zambia. It is also rich in comparative references to other African working classes. This work is a major contribution to scholarship on the labour movement in colonial Zambia.

My study in a sense seeks to pick the story of the Zambian working class as a whole where Meebelo left off, that is 1964. It wont, however be as detailed or as theoretically tight as Meebelo's. It should thus be regarded as an outline to be filled with more meat later on.

Another weakness in the studies of the working class in Zambia and which this study does not correct, is the neglect of the rural workers and the peasantry in general.[2] Farm Labour as well as the peasantry played an important political role during the struggle for independence. In the post-colonial era the produce of the countryside generated by farm labour and the peasantry have to a great extent subsidized urban consumption particularly that of the various petty bourgeoisies and bourgeoisies. Datta states that labour on the large agricultural estates in Zambia, encouraged since the 1970s in response to internal and external pressures, remains among the most exploited, with little organized protest by the workers (or intellectuals) and in contrast to Zimbabwe, with almost no 'protectionist' state intervention.[3] This exploitation should be reflected in studies like those reflecting the struggles of the mineworkers. It is hoped that someday someone will document the state of the rural workers and peasantry from the colonial days to the present. The struggles of rural workers and peasantry will be felt in the future given the apparent shift in state policies towards the rural sector. I also do not deal with the very important role of women workers in Zambia, another weakness in the studies of class struggles in Zambia.

The last major weakness of most studies on the Zambian working class is the failure to pinpoint the theoretical framework informing the Zambian state in matters of industrial relations. What is this framework? And why this framework? How has it been implemented? Is it consistently applied? etc. Thus while a number of authors would like to tell us that the Zambian working class (particularly the mineworkers) behave like a labour aristocracy, they are not prepared to tell us why the state behaves in a certain way towards the working class. They have no developed theory of the state and its relationship to the working class.

I will suggest here the framework informing the Zambian state.

The Zambian state seems to be influenced by the "pluralist" theory of industrial relations at least in its controlled form. I will show how the various institutional set ups in Zambia reflect this theory of industrial relations. The central tenets of pluralism are plotted in Table 1.1. The pluralists do acknowledge the existence of industrial conflict between workers and managers. But they aim at containing this conflict.

For the pluralists, the solution to industrial conflict is collective bargaining. For them, collective bargaining is seen as having historically eradicated the most blatant economic inequities of nineteenth and early twentieth century laissez-fair capitalism. It still helps to eradicate some of the worst excesses of capitalist society. Further, for them collective bargaining ensures that union and management are joint authors of their rules. This ensures the existence of "industrial democracy" which corresponds to the existence of "political democracy" in the larger society. And lastly, collective bargaining is seen as ensuring the institutionalization of industrial conflict. This means that, conflict cannot get out of hand and this is good for both union and management. If conflict gets out of hand, pluralists accept the occurrence of strikes but these strikes must be within manageable limits so that they do not disrupt unnecessarily the productive system. Strikes are necessary for their cathartic value which ultimately bring order and stability to industrial relations and society as a whole.[4]

Pluralism which is but the same as liberalism portrays the state as a subject, the objective arbitrator and great leveler above and beyond the mass of social interaction. The state is then portrayed as a neutral, if pluralist subject, capable of incorporating and accommodating a wealth of diverse social desires and interests. The role of the state in conflict is to create conditions and atmosphere for peaceful resolution of conflict. The state does not itself partake in this conflict. The state however plays but a complex and often times a different role.[5] According to the marxist framework the state plays a fundamental role in class struggles. According to the general Marxist observations,[6] the state becomes involved in organizing struggles – in confining them within limits or repressing them – so that they do not threaten capitalist relations of production. It does this by disorganizing the dominated classes, which it

Table 1.1

Three Perspectives on Industrial Relations

View of:	Unitary	Pluralist	Radical
1. Workplace Conflict	deviant; inappropriate	within limits normal	fundamental conflict; endemic under capitalist-mode of production
2. Power Balance	not relevant	rough equivalence or at least no duress	gross imbalance in favour of management
3. Workplace Hierarchy	natural, necessary	necessary, though scope for more employee participation	repressive; denies role of employee as producer
4. Collective Bargaining	not acceptable, nor necessary, management acts in interests of all parties	limited shared decision-making mainly on economic and personnel issue both acceptable and desirable	employees only successful concerning 'marginal' issues; power balance remains essentially unaltered
5. Role of Labour Law	limited, work relationship essentially a private matter; reinforce management authority	place limits upon arbitrary exercise of managerial discretion; ensures rough equivalence of bargaining power etc.	maintains managerial dominance; in work-lace; fails to ensure significant substantive justice for employees
6. Role of Grievance Arbitration	none	keep conflict within reasonable bounds' adjudicate disputes between parties	amount to denial of right to withdraw labour during course of agreement; only marginal, individual protections provided
7. Supporting Cultural Values	private property, contract, business efficiency, expertise	business efficiency, industrial democracy, voluntarism, public interest	

accomplishes by transforming relations among agents of production (capitalists, managers, workers, etc.) into relations among individuals constituted as citizens with equal rights before the law, education and in the electoral system, or into relations among parties, races, religious groups, or language groups. In this way, the apparatus of the state appear to be above classes or autonomous with respect to classes, in that they operate according to their own logic, which cannot be arbitrarily changed at the will of any one class. Moreover, this autonomy constitutes both a real and a necessary basis for preserving the political interests of capitalists – that is their class interest in the maintenance of the capitalist order. For, to preserve these political interests the state must frequently act against the capitalists' economic interests by granting concessions to the other classes. In normal times the state applies coercion in a more or less legally prescribed manner and not at the immediate behest of the dominant class; but in times of crisis the state may lose its relative autonomy and become an instrument of the dominant class in the arbitrary repression of class struggle.[7]

In this study, we will see how the Zambian state has been involved in direct struggle against the working class while strenuously trying to appear autonomous from ongoing class struggles. On more occasions than not, the state has bared its teeth and repressed the working class on behalf of the dominant class interests.

Labour Policies in Zambia

To get a feel of some of the issues I will expand upon later I will summarize a few studies here that offer frameworks in which industrial relations in Zambia have been organized. There are basically three identifiable interpretations of the effects of labour policies in Zambia: first, the perspective that sees the (attempted) incorporation of labour by the state in Zambia.[8] Second, the perspective which sees periods of incorporation especially of the "labour aristocracy" by the state and periods of increasing autonomy of labour.[9] Thirdly, the perspective which holds that incorporation has failed in the face of labour struggles for autonomy and assertiveness.[10]

Fincham and Zulu detail what appear to be three aspects of labour's attempted incorporation in Zambia: first, state centralization of trade union power by creating ZCTU in 1965, second, the informal incorporation of trade union leadership into a national development policy – through political appointments, offers of higher salaries etc., and third, through trade union legislation i.e. the enactment of the Industrial Relations Act (IRA) in 1971 which among others provided for the affiliation of all unions to the ZCTU, the creation of the Industrial Relations Court (IRC) and Works Councils (WCs). Were Fincham and Zulu to accept these attempted institutional arrangements at their face value, this would be a formalistic interpretation of incorporation as it would regard formal arrangements as achieving their aims. Fincham and Zulu's analysis is far from accepting this formalism as they show in their data which will be explored later. The situation is more complex than it appears.

Parpart and Shaw specify the conditions under which labour became incorporated, namely the availability of copper revenues to share between the various fractions of the bourgeoisie (international and local) and labour during the first ten years or so of independence and the collapse of the alliance between the state bureaucratic bourgeoisie and the "labour aristocracy" when the economy entered a crisis period in the mid-seventies. Thus in the late seventies and into the eighties, labour has been increasingly becoming militant in a political sense against the state, according to Parpart and Shaw. Michael Burawoy in his popular monograph, *The Colour of Class on the Copper Mines* written in the early seventies was the first to show the relationship between the State's labour policies and copper mineworkers. This will be explored more fully later.

Bates documents the state's attempts at incorporating labour to its socially defined economic development priorities and social justice principles and assesses whether these attempts were successful and what factors determined their outcome. He concludes that these attempts failed due to union strength and the strategic location and concentration of the labour force in the country's main foreign exchange earner i.e. copper. These factors limited the state's ability to coerce labour i.e. Mining labour.

According to Bates, the Zambian state's labour policy towards the mineworkers was informed at least up to 1971 when the study appeared by two overriding concerns: rapid economic development and the principle of social justice. The first concern had four components to it: discipline of the work force; obedience of the work force to the supervisors; abandonment of the strike policy and lastly wage restraint on the part of the work force. Given the preponderant contribution of the copper revenues to the overall economic development of Zambia, if the mineworkers were disciplined, they obeyed their supervisors, only went on strike as a last resort and restrained their wage demands in keeping with labour productivity, then more copper revenues would be available to finance economic development. Thus went the argument. The state went about ensuring that the above defined labour policy and its components were adhered to by the mineworkers. This was done through exhortation; joint state-management and labour seminars; pressure and force on the mineworkers union etc.

Concern for social justice informed the second government labour policy. The copper industry was foreign owned and practiced discriminatory policies e.g. expatriate workers were earning eight times more than the Africans. This was more or less the same in manufacturing and agriculture. To move away from racial disparities in terms of income, state labour policy in the field of social justice had three components: rapid Zambianization; the equalization of amenities and an incomes policy all of which would remove racial disparities in this field. If these were achieved, then social justice would have been achieved. Thus the state went about trying to implement these three components of social justice labour policy.

Before I move on to assessing the response of the working class I must comment on one thing. Bates accepts uncritically the state's alleged commitment to rapid economic development. He states for example, "it is difficult to overemphasize the level of the government's commitment to rapid economic development".[11] This belief was engendered by the government's estimates of the growth rates it sought in the first development plan: 63% in the mines; 117% in commerce; 146% in manufacturing; 147% in services and 198% in construction. These were indeed very high estimates but says nothing about who was to bear the burden.

The implication could be that if it is accepted that the government is committed to rapid economic development then its labour policies no matter what their colouration is, so long they are seen to be geared toward the promotion of economic development they should be implicitly if not explicitly accepted by the labour movement and anybody else for that matter. Later on I shall discuss how the mineworkers and other segments of the working class behaved in light of the state's desire to turn them from a "consumptionist" to a "productionist" orientation.[12]

Labour Aristocracy in Zambia

Nsolo Mijere is one of the latest scholars to discuss at length the mineworkers as constituting a labour aristocracy.[13] The centrepiece of Mijere's discussion is the rejection of the government's decentralization policy of 1980 by the Mineworkers Union of Zambia. Mijere constructs three hypotheses to explain the MUZ's rejection of decentralization: (a) because MUZ constitutes a labour aristocracy and thus they wanted to preserve their privileged position; (b) they wanted to prevent UNIP (United National Independence Party – the ruling party since 1964) from concentrating power in its hands which would be detrimental to the interests and power of MUZ, and (c) they also wanted to prevent the increasing alliance and concomitantly growing political and economic power of the political elites in Zambia and international capital.[14]

I dispute the first and last hypotheses. I think while it is true that economically the mineworkers constitute a labour aristocracy, it does not follow that politically they are conservative on every issue. On the issue of decentralization, I will show later that they were motivated more by the fear of loss of autonomy and democratic control than on defending their aristocratic position. It is arguable whether UNIP imposed decentralization in order to bring about more democracy. The workers thought the policy was aimed at imposing further dictatorship. For me this rejection of decentralization implies critical class struggle between the working class and the political class. It means a fundamental clash over how to reorganize society, for what purposes and for whose gain.

Stephen Chan puts the aristocratic nature of the mineworkers in more emphatic terms:

> The copper miners form the most powerful union – since they handle the nation's single most precious commodity. They are unlike the other unions in that they constitute a labour aristocracy. They are not representative of the nations's workers, because their strategic position attracts for them special considerations and privileges. Moreover, the mines are located in a specific geographical area, and the miners have a specific tribal base which the nation's leadership cannot afford to ignore. The militancy and success of the miners is, therefore, atypical.[15]

The short-coming with this otherwise sound analysis is the failure to recognize the contribution of this so-called labour aristocracy to the strengthening of the labour movement as a whole, particularly in its interaction with the ZCTU. Why should workers not use their special strategic location to advance their interests and by demonstration effect the position of other workers? It is to be remembered that without a strong MUZ and perhaps also without a strong ZCTU to act as countervailing forces to the omnipotent party machinery, Zambia would probably have an entrenched and secure dictatorship. In fact this is the whole point to this study, to show that the class struggles waged by the Zambian working class headed by ZCTU and MUZ explain to a large extent the continued existence of a fragile third world-type democracy in Zambia. It is not the product of accident or benevolent leadership. It is embedded in Zambia's political and economic history.

Notes

1. Lusaka: Kenneth Kaunda, 1986.

2. For a broader commentary on this, see Kusum Datta, "Farm Labour, Agrarian Capital and the State in Colonial Zambia: The African Labour Corps, 1942 - 52" *Journal of Southern African Studies* Vol. 14, No. 3 (April 1988) pp. 371-392.

3. Datta *ibid* p. 371.

4. See Geoffrey England, "Some Observations on Selected Strike Laws" in Kenneth Swan and Katherine Swinton (eds.) *Studies in Labour Law* (Toronto: Butterworths, 1983) pp. 223-298. See also Andrew Goldsmith, "Three Models of Management Labour Relations" *Osgoode Hall Law Journal* (Forthcoming).

5. For a critique of pluralism, see Ralph Miliband, *The State in Capitalist Society* (New York: Basic Books, 1969).

6. See Antonio Gramsci, *Selection from Prison Notebooks* (New York: International Publishers, 1971); Nicos Poulantzas, *Political Power and Social Classes* (London: New Left Books, 1973);

7. Michael Burawoy, *Manufacturing Consent* (Chicago and London: The University of Chicago Press, 1979) pp. 196-197.

8. Robin Fincham and Grace Zulu "Labour and Participation in Zambia" in *Development in Zambia*, edited by Ben Turok, (London: Zed, 1981) pp. 214-227.

9. Jane Parpart and Timothy Shaw, "Contradiction and Coalition: Class Fractions in Zambia, 1964 to 1984" *Africa Today* 30, 3, 1983, pp. 23-51.

10. Robert Bates, *Unions, Parties and Political Development: A Study of Mineworkers in Zambia*, (New Haven and London: Yale University Press, 1971).

11. Ibid., p.27. Michael Burawoy has pointed out that Bates has uncritically accepted the Government's ideological rationalizations to control labour, see "Another Look at the Mineworker" *African Social Research* 14, 1972, pp.239-287.

12. See Bates, note 10 for use of these concepts.

13. "The Mineworkers' Resistance to Governmental Decentralization in Zambia: Nation-Building and Labour Aristocracy in the Third World" (Ph.D. Dissertation, Branders University, 1986).

14. Ibid pp. 32-34.

15. Stephen Chan, "Humanism, Intellectuals and the Left in Zambia", in Kwaku Osei-Hwedie and Muna Ndulo, (eds.) *Issues in Zambian Development* (Nyangwe and Roxbury: Omenana, 1985).

3

Class Formation and Class Struggles in Colonial Zambia:

Brief Summary of the Political
Economy of Zambia in Historic
Perspective

Z ambia was incorporated into the world economy as a company state
beginning from the end of the 19th Century. The Company, British South
Africa Company (BSA Co.) had been given mineral rights over the
territory. In the course of time a small settler community developed which took
to farming. This settler community, blossoming into an agrarian capitalist class
was later joined by representatives of mining capital who came to operate the
copper mines when they became operational in the 1920s. The latter constituted themselves as an imperial bourgeoisie. With the handing over of the
company state to the British colonial government in 1924, a colonial state
apparatus proper was erected. Although manned by settlers, it was controlled
by the colonial office in London. The colonial state catered to the interests of
the settler bourgeoisie as well as to those of the mining imperial bourgeoisie.
Thus at this time there were two fractions of the bourgeoisie, agricultural
(settler) and imperial (mining) with a cotery of bureaucrats, some seconded
from the colonial office, staffing the state institutions alongside the settler

bourgeoisie. The colonial state was thus the state of the settler and imperial bourgeoisies. It acted at their behest as any analysis of labour policies would reveal. Attending the development of settler agriculture, mining and railways, was the development of an African peasantry as well as an African working class. We shall not talk about the peasantry here but confine our remarks to the working class. This working class was constituted in three stages, the first stage (roughly before 1900) saw its birth as forced labour, the second stage (about 1900s to the 1940s) as migrant labour and the third stage (1940s to 1960s and beyond) as stabilized labour. A European working class was also employed in the skilled jobs (due to the existence of the colour bar system) in the mining companies thus constituting two sections of the working class in the mines: African and European.

A labour regime to acquire and control labour accompanied each of the successive stages of the constitution of the African working class: naked force was used during the first stage (forced labour); indirect force in the form of hut and poll tax to drive Africans to work was used during the second stage. Some form of labour legislation with penal sanctions was developed later during this period i.e. Employment of Natives Ordinance in 1929. The third stage saw a cotery of labour legislation and labour laws as well as the sanction of African trade unions by the colonial state. Labour legislation and the sanctioning of trade unions was in response to working class struggles. Penal sanctions and brutal repression accompanied working class struggles during this period. Working class struggles were aimed at; *(a)* the abolition of discriminatory wages whereby European workers earned more than African workers, *(b)* protesting the industrial colour bar, *(c)* higher wages, *(d)* improved working conditions, and *(e)* removing racial humiliation generally. The African working class sponsored massive strikes during the thirties, forties and fifties addressing the above issues.

An African petty bourgeoisie emerged also as a result of industrial growth and the expansion of government service during the forties and fifties which took to nationalist politics as well as trade unionism.

At independence in 1964, it is the nationalist petty bourgeois fraction that inherited state power and using wealth accrued through economic reforms, easy loans from state coffers, corruption, free housing, cars, fridges and high salaries etc. constituted itself as a "bureaucratic bourgeoisie". It is this class that inherited certain pieces of labour legislation and also enacted its own. It is this class which through nationalization of economic enterprises etc. came to control large slices of economic life of the nation and hence to confront directly the working class, represented by the other wing of the African petty bourgeoisie, also nurtured by colonialism.

Theory and History of the Development of the Zambian Working Class

E. P. Thompson calls the process that accompanied the coming into being of the English working class as "making", "making ... (as) an active process, which owes as much to agency as to conditioning. The (English) working class did not rise like the sun at an appointed time. It was present at its own making".[1] Perhaps not as a working class proper. His notion of "making" is quite relevant to the situation in Zambia, as elsewhere, as we will show below. Karl Marx has perhaps more than any other scholar described more vividly the violent process that engendered the birth, making and development of the (English) working class.[2] The process was ignited by an external agency, acting at that time on an unformed but by no means absent working class. As Thompson remarks the working class was present at its own making. The initial process of the "making" of the (classical) working class, from the 15th to the 18th century, Marx called "primitive accumulation", the historical process of divorcing the producer from the means of production".[3]

The 'freed' population was then available for unmitigated exploitation in the budding urban industry and at this time, "the demand for wage-labour grew ... rapidly with every accumulation of capital, whilst the supply of wage-labour followed but slowly".[4] Lack of enough wage-labour meant more expropriations of means of production from the peasant farmers. A great "advantage" which accrued from expropriating the agricultural population was the creation and expansion of the home market.[5]

Capitalism was the first economic system to separate industry from agriculture hence expanding the division of labour. The classic example of the capitalist route is of course England, with variations elsewhere, in Europe, Russia,[6] South Africa,[7] Rhodesia,[8] Kenya[9] etc.

The divorce of the peasantry from their means of production under classical capitalism was more thorough than it later became under what I call the "colonial-capitalist" route. This route involved "partial destruction" and "partial preservation" of the "peasant mode of production" depending on the needs of colonial capital.[10] The destructive aspect involved the "freeing" of the agricultural population for mine, settlerfarm, railway-building and etc. employment. The mechanisms for "freeing" labour included political (coercive) and economic means, e.g. seizure of land and livestock, compulsion of peasants, conversion of conquered peoples to slaves and wage-slavery, payment of taxes, commodity production etc. This "free labour" was engaged by capital as migrant labour so that the cost of reproduction could be met in the rural areas.

Labour migrancy became a very important ingredient for colonial capitalist development. Samir Amin has identified Southern and Central Africa as the "Africa of Labour Reserves". The oft-cited statement of his, reads:

> The terms in which most of the African People of most of the areas of Southern and Central Africa have been integrated into the world economy has been through labour migration rather than the direct production of commodities. In all the countries immediately to the North of the Zambezi, as well as the well-known examples to the South, not only have large numbers of African men come as *Gaster Beiter* in mines, farms and industries controlled by whites and run as capitalist production units, but the communities from which these migrants have come have become geared to the production and reproduction of this special form of exported labour power.[11]

The "partial preservation" aspect involved leaving some regions on their own, more or less intact, while others were transformed into commodity producing areas (plantation and settlerfarms) employing "free" peasant labour, e.g. the Gezira Scheme in Sudan, Kilimanjaro Region in Northeastern Tanzania, and Murang'a District in Central Kenya.[12] Some peasants responded to the "pull of market forces" by engaging in commodity production.

This partial destruction and partial preservation of colonial capitalism and the concomitant migrant labour system resulted in what has been called the development of semi-proletarian labour – half workers and half peasants. This system of making of a working class had a tremendous effect on the nature and development of class struggles in colonial Africa.[13] However the changing needs of colonial capital required the presence of a permanent labour force whose existence gave rise to the modification of the nature and character of class struggles in the latter part of the colonial era.

This chapter examines the making of the Zambian working class and the class struggles this working class engaged against the colonial state and capital on the one hand and the instruments of class struggle deployed by the colonial state and capital against the working class on the other hand. At the centre of this analysis will be the impact of economic processes on the nature and character of class struggle in colonial Zambia.

Primitive Accumulation and Early Colonialism in Northern Rhodesia

Northern Rhodesia, as Zambia was called prior to independence in 1964, was formerly colonized in 1889 by the British South Africa Company (BSA Co.)

under Charter from the English Crown.[14] The BSA Co. under John Cecil Rhodes who had made fortunes in mining in the South hoped that mineral resources would also be discovered in the North. At its formation in 1889, the aims of the BSA Co. was stated as follows:

1. "To extend the railway and telegraph systems northwards in the direction of the Zambezi".

2. "To encourage emigration and colonization".

3. "To promote trade and commerce".

4. "To develop and work mineral and other concessions under the management of one powerful organization, thereby obviating conflicts and complications between the various interests that have been acquired within the region and securing to the native chiefs and their subjects the rights reserved to them under several concessions".[15]

Thereafter, the BSA Co. supposedly obtained a concession from a local King, King Lewanika in North Western Rhodesia to engage in mining activities, among others:

1. To carry on any manufacturing commercial or other trading business.

2. To search for dig win and keep diamonds gold coal oil and all other precious stones minerals or substances.

3. To construct improve equip work and manage public works railways tramways roads bridges lighting water-works and all other works and conveniences of general or public utility.

4. To carry on the business of banking in all its branches.

5. To buy sell refine manipulate mint and deal in precious stones specie coin and all other metals and minerals.

6. To manufacture and import arms and ammunition of all kinds.

7. To do all such things as are incidental or conducive to the exercise attainment or protection of all or any of the rights powers and concessions hereby granted. And to grant to the British South Africa Company administrative rights to deal with adjudicate upon all cases between white men and between white men and natives it being clearly understood that all cases between natives shall be left to the King to deal with and dispose of.[16]

However, the BSA Co.'s dreams of building another mining empire in Northern Rhodesia were not immediately realised. It soon became clear that the low-grade ores discovered at Broken Hill in Central Northern Rhodesia and Ndola in the Northwest would never yield significant profits. Thus, instead of turning Northern Rhodesia into a mining enclave, Company officials began to see Northern Rhodesia as a labour reserve for mines in Southern Rhodesia and Katanga in the Congo. In order to force Africans into wage labour, the Company levied taxes and permitted corporate recruiting. It also encouraged white farmers and traders to settle in the territory to supply food and trade goods to the mines.[17] Although the influx of farmers was very slow in the early years and never really picked up until after the Second World War, the minimal numbers still entailed the eviction of Africans from their ancestral homes. The Company as well as colonial administrators (from 1924 when the Company relinquished control of Northern Rhodesia), embarked on a deliberate policy of creating native reserves and alienating the best lands for European farmers.[18] This policy of primitive accumulation yielded an influx of migrant labourers to the mines in the South and Katanga. The greatest impact of land alienation and native reserves was felt in three areas: along the line of rail (the railway reached Livingstone in 1904, Broken Hill in 1906 and the would-be Copperbelt afterwards), around Fort Jameson in the East and around Mbala in the North, where concentrations of European commercial farming developed.[19] The railway brought the first great influx of white farmers. As is the case all over the world, the development of transport is the locomotion of economic development.

Taxation was another method of primitive accumulation that was pretty successful in driving Africans to the farms and mines of Southern Rhodesia, South Africa and Katanga. As early as 1899, Codrington, the Deputy Administrator of North Eastern Rhodesia complained that "Labour ... was extremely difficult to obtain".[20] Codrington claimed that the African was a free man. He had indeed never been as free. He paid no taxes and worked only when his own inclination so decided. The Company decided henceforth to break that cycle of freedom by introducing poll and hut taxes between 1900 and 1904. The tax was specifically intended by the administrators of Northern Rhodesia to produce a steady flow of labour without resorting to legal compulsion. As L. H. Gann has observed, "Taxation gave an enormous impetus to migration. It created a regular, instead of a seasonal demand for cash, and extended that demand over the whole of the Territory, not just areas near to labour centres".[21] Codrington seems to have forgotten the massive forced labour which included burning of huts, preceding the imposition of taxes. Forced labour was the initial tool of primitive accumulation and it yielded small amounts of labour.

Migrant Labourers as Semi-Proletarians

Those Africans who left their lands to seek work elsewhere had to be channelled properly. This task was met by the regularization of recruitment procedures. In 1903 a Native Labour Bureau was created and granted the exclusive right to recruit labour North of the Zambezi River for employment in Southern Rhodesia. Other agents recruited workmen for employment in Northern Rhodesia and the Congo. In 1930, the colonial government forced the recruiting companies to form a unified labour recruitment mechanism, which resulted in the formation of the Native Labour Association. Right up to the early thirties all labourers recruited were engaged as migrant workers. The practice was employment for six months and then back to the village. Those workers who presented themselves without passing through the properly constituted recruitment procedures were employed on a one-monthly basis.[22] This class of migrant workers gave rise to what has been called a class of "semi-proletarians"[23] or according to Helmuth Heisler, a transitional class of proletarianized peasants that he terms a class of "target-proletarians".[24] This class of working people depended upon a combination of wages and farm incomes for their livelihoods. According to Richard Sklar, low wages, lack of job security for Africans and consequently, the perpetuation of migrant labour delayed the inevitable formation of a true proletarian – in the Marxian sense – a class of persons who are primarily if not exclusively dependent upon wage labour.[25] Migrant labour system was a deliberate policy of the colonial state and capital to maintain low wages, thus extracting super profits and also to control the inevitable class struggles that would result from permanent proletarianization or a stabilized work force. With the development of the copper mining industry, the development of a permanent proletariat was inevitable.

The Copper Industry: From Semi-Proletarians to a Permanent Proletariat

Copper mining in Northern Rhodesia began in earnest in the early twenties and was firmly established by 1926. The immediate stimulant of copper mining was the phenomenal increases in copper prices after the First World War. Copper was in high demand. However, labour supply to the copperbelt had to compete with the already established routes to Katanga, Southern Rhodesia and South Africa, as well as to established commercial farming enclaves along the line of rail, around Mbala and Fort Jameson. By 1929 for example, Katanga had absorbed some 10,500 Northern Rhodesian workers.[26]

As in the mines of Katanga and the South, initial labourers were engaged as migrant labourers. Due to labour shortages, direct recruitment was still the normal practice throughout the twenties. Labour recruitment was very successful. In 1927, there were 11,000 Africans employed in the mines and these had increased to 30,000 by 1930.

The rapid development of the copper industry and the rapid proletarianization was halted by the Depression of 1929 to the early thirties. Suddenly there was an influx of workers who were laid off in the mines of Katanga and the South and increasing unemployment within the copperbelt. Nchanga Consolidated Copper Mines Ltd. and Mufulira Mine closed during the Depression and Nchanga paid no dividends to Shareholders for thirteen years. Roan Antelope did not declare a dividend until 1935. That is how bad the situation was and inevitably this slowed down the pace of proletarianization on the copper-belt and occasioned what Marx called a "surplus population" which takes three forms in the urban industrial sector under the capitalist mode of production: the floating, the latent and the stagnant.[27] From the peak of 30,000 African employees in 1930, employment dropped to 18,000 Africans in 1931 and 7,000 in 1932. By 1939 employment of Africans had not even reached the 1930 level. There were only 26,000 African employees. There was indeed a "surplus population" on the copperbelt. The floating "surplus population" is that which is both attracted and repelled by modern inventions of machinery. Once a new factory is opened, more labour is required but once machinery is introduced, part of the labour force is discharged. This is the section that floats around. Normally it is of the younger generation. At the time of the Depression, Northern Rhodesia Copper Mining executives were debating whether or not to replace labour with machines.

The latent "surplus population" is that portion which is thrown up by the introduction of capitalist production in agriculture. This population is always on the move to the urban areas looking for better opportunities. This movement makes it appear that there is a latent surplus population in the countryside. This is because, "as soon as capitalist production takes possession of agriculture, and in proportion to the extent to which it does so, the demand for an agricultural labouring population falls absolutely, while accumulation of the capital employed in agriculture advances, without this repulsion being, as in none-agricultural industries, compensated by a greater attraction". Hence "part of the agricultural population is therefore constantly on the point of passing over into an urban or manufacturing proletariat, and on the look-out for circumstances favourable to this transformation".[28] In Northern Rhodesia, "passing over" was compelled by forced labour, taxation, recruitment as well as alienation of land thereby forcing Africans onto the urban areas.

The stagnant "surplus population" forms a part of the active labour army but with extremely irregular employment. It "furnishes to capital an inexhaustible reservoir of disposable labour power".[29] The Depression indeed created a stagnant "surplus population" on the copperbelt. It is not surprising that labour recruitment ended during the Depression.

Migrant labour however could not sustain a specialized and technical undertaking like copper mining. Further, unlike gold mining, copper cannot be profitably produced by unskilled (and migrant) labour in small mining operations. Rather, it depends on having sufficient accessible high-grade ore, enough capital to develop it, and a reliable skilled labour force capable of mining and producing the copper. While mining companies strive to minimize costs, one way of minimizing costs efficiently is by improving labour skills and then rationalizing labour through improved technology. According to Parpart, this constant need to upgrade the skills of copper miners (especially after the Depression) shaped corporate labour policies of the mining companies. It led to stabilization and expansion of African skills, and eventually to the substitution of some African miners for more expensive European mine labour. European workers had more privileges e.g. in terms of housing, salaries and all other amenities than African workers. All of these developments had important implications for the development of the Northern Rhodesian working class.[30]

One of the consequences of the stabilization of the workforce – permanent proletarianization was the development of collective organization and action by the African working class. Prior to the stabilization of the African working class, there was hardly any collective resistance to capital.

Proletarianization and Class Struggles, 1930s to 1964

From the above review, it can be seen that class struggles in colonial Zambia can best be studied by looking at the situation in the copper industry. This is where labour and capital were concentrated and naturally has been the focus of many studies as a result of this concentration. Copper was the locomotion of the Northern Rhodesian political economy. Later industries were built largely from the copper revenues.

As already stated, because of the migrant labour system, a permanent proletariat was prevented from developing. Capital deliberately tended to treat labour as constituted of "tribesmen".[31] Even after signs of permanent proletarianization were visible, capital still regarded the African working class as mere tribesmen. This further justified the refusal to permit the formation of African trade unions, despite some impetus in the colonial office in London favouring the formation of tightly controlled African trade unions.[32]

To represent these "tribesmen", mining capital introduced a Council of Tribal Elders, chosen by and from various ethnic groups, first at Roan Antelope

Mine in 1931. The Councils of Tribal Elders were to be the official spokesmen for the African workers, they were also empowered to perform judicial functions in petty cases, mainly domestic disputes involving African customary law.[33] However, even without "proper" trade unions to represent the interests of the African workers, these workers were still able to organize massive strikes in 1935 and 1940.[34] The Commission that was set up to investigate the causes of the 1935 strike concluded the causes of the strike as:[35]

1. The increase in taxation in the mining areas, and the timing and implementation of the announcement of this increase.

2. Alleged grievances by African miners concerning wages, rations, deductions and their treatment by European workers.

3. Great numbers of unemployed in the mining areas.

4. Detribalization.

5. Inadequate government contact with the mining compounds.

6. The influence of organizations active in the compounds, such as the Watch Tower Movement and the Mbeni Dance Society.

A workers' poster at Nkana Mine put the causes of the strike in simple basic terms as a struggle against lower wages, taxation and inhuman treatment by mine management:[36]

Listen to this all who live in the country, think well how they treat us and to ask for a land. Do we live in good treatment, no; therefore let us ask one another and remember this treatment. Because we wish on the day of 29th, April, every person not to work, he who will go to work, and if we see him, it will be a serious case. Know how they cause us to suffer, they cheat us for money, they arrest us for loafing, they persecute and put us in goal for tax. What reason have we done? Secondly, do you not wish to hear these words, well listen this year of 1935, if they will not increase us more money stop paying tax, do you think they can kill you, no. Let us encourage surely you will see that God will be with us. See how we suffer with the work and how we are continually reviled and beaten underground. Many brothers of us die for 22s. 6d., is this money that we should lose our lives for. He who cannot read should tell his companion that on the 29th, April not to go to work. These words do not come from here, they come from the wisers who are far away and enable to encourage us. That all. Hear well if it is right let us do so. We are all of the Nkana Africans men and women.

This strike was brutally put down. As usual the colonial state came to the aid of mining capital by sending in the army and police to shoot down the strikers. Six African miners were shot down and several dozens were wounded. The mining company did not even pretend to listen to the grievances of the miners. Hence the strike brought absolutely no material rewards.[37] For many scholars, the significance of the 1935 strike lies in the "consciousness" displayed by African workers, consciousness of their collective interests and collective exploitation at the hands of mining capital.[38] This consciousness went beyond that of the African Welfare Associations that started in the 1920s and started the impetus for political organizations. These African Welfare Associations are discussed in detail in Henry Meebelo's *Reaction to Colonialism* and I need not deal with them here. But this strike is regarded also as the concerted starting point of Zambian modern political consciousness, the purveyor of nationalist politics. Another significant development which showed the insensitivity and intransigence of mining capital to the demands of African workers was that although the tribal elders were ineffective before and during the 1935 (and 1940) strikes, the system of tribal representation was extended throughout the copperbelt and redesignated as "Tribal Representative" system. Thus capital was still treating the African workers not as a class of workers but instead, as a collectivity of tribesmen. It was obviously an ideological tool of class struggle on the part of mining capital.

In 1940, the African mine workers came out again on another, this time more co-ordinated and widespread strike, concerning more or less the same grievances as the 1935 strike.[39] The State again came to the aid of capital, sending in military reinforcements which led to the shooting down of seventeen African strikers. The workers in the end received less than one percent of their wage demands.[40] These strikes caused the Government as well as mining companies to seek means of preventing violent strikes, by directing African grievances into controllable channels.[41] African workers wanted trade unions. Mine management and the government preferred Tribal Elders to represent African interests. So they extended this system. But class struggle had entered firmly in industrial relations in Northern Rhodesia. There was on the other hand, mining capital and the colonial state and the African working class on the other hand. The African working class sought their own permanent vehicle or organization of class struggle – trade union organization. Throughout most of the forties, the colonial office in London and the local colonial state and mining capital resisted the formation of African Trade Unions. This was also typical of the rest of colonial Africa. European mineworkers were allowed to form a trade union in 1936, one year after the massive strike organized by African workers in 1935. Failing to prevent forever the inexorable motion towards the emergence of African trade unionism, the colonial state and capital decided to mould the nature of African trade unionism that would emerge. In the mid-forties, a labour Officer, a William Comrie was appointed by the Labour Government of Britain to oversee the formation of African trade unions. Thus emerged the African Mineworkers Unions throughout the Copperbelt mines in 1948. These merged to form the African Mine Workers' Union (AMWU) in 1949. This union and others were modelled along British trade unionism, with two cardinal principles: to stick to trade unionism i.e. to matters of collective bargaining and general welfare of the workers and secondly, to stay out of politics. These were principles that would influence a great deal the emergent African trade unions and their relations with capital and the emergent African nationalist politics.[42] They were also to influence the relations between labour and the state in the post colonial era.

Trade unions were strictly to be guided by labour laws that were enacted at the time that trade unions were allowed to exist. In 1949, the Trade Unions and Trade Disputes Ordinance was enacted. It spelled out what is known as collective bargaining in industrial relations in Zambia – the employers and workers meeting at the table with more or less equal power and to equally represent their respective interests. A "pluralist model" of industrial relations was in the making. That same year the Industrial Conciliation Ordinance was also passed. In 1948, Wages, Wages Councils and Conditions of Employment Ordinance was passed. All these pieces of legislation had to do with the regulation of modern industrial relations whereas the two previous pieces of legislation i.e. Employment Natives Ordinance of 1929 and Employment of Natives (Amendment) Ordinance of 1940 had to do with regulation of migrant labourers, the honouring of contracts and punishment for breach of contract etc. The later labour legislation stayed in the books for some years after independence.

The formation of AMWU opened the way for the formation of other African trade unions in other undertakings. The key issues for which they organized were increased wages, improved work conditions, African advancement and an end to the industrial colour bar.

By 1954 sixteen African unions had been formed. By independence in 1964, key unions had been born and some of them became forerunners to future unions: AMWU with a membership of 19,000 in 1949; Northern Rhodesia African Railway Workers Trade Union (NRARWTU) formed in 1950; National Union of Building, Engineering and General Workers (NUBEGW) registered in 1960 which evolved from General Workers Union formed in 1947; National Union of Commercial and Industrial Workers (NUCIW) registered in 1960 which evolved from Shop Assistant's Union formed in 1947, National Union of Public Services Workers (NUPSW) registered in 1960; National Union of Local Authority Workers (NULAW) registered in 1961;

Zambia National Union of Teachers (ZNUT) registered in 1962. By 1964 there were twenty-nine unions with a total membership of 101,654 members.

Collective organization of workers inevitably led to collective action against management. The mineworkers went into rapid succession strikes against management for wages in 1952, 1955 and 1956. The 1952 strike went on for three weeks and achieved wage increases for the mineworkers; the 1955 went on for ten weeks and saw 33,000 out of 37,000 workers go on strike and 1956 saw a series of rolling strikes which seriously interrupted the industry.

The colonial state intervened in 1956 to protect capital. A state of emergency was proclaimed, the first of several; forty union leaders were arrested and detained; and trade union legislation was amended to introduce greater governmental control. The Government regarded these stern measures to have brought to an end the phase of "militant unionism".[43] For a few years this appeared to be the case until the mineworkers went on strike in 1962 and the teachers in 1963. This same period, 1956 to 1964 saw countryside political agitation for independence organized by African nationalists.

An impression should not be created that only the mineworkers went on strikes during the colonial era. Other workers also went on strikes. Meebelo in his book, *African Proletarians And Colonial Capitalism* documents at length the struggles of other workers. For example, major strikes were conducted by the Zambezi Sawmills Workers in 1943 and the Rhodesian Railway Workers in 1945 and so on.

Class Struggle and Nationalism

One cardinal principle was accepted both by Union leaders and rank and file; that the primary function of the union was raising wages and the improvement of working conditions through collective bargaining and if necessary strike action. Thus trade union activity was (theoretically) separated from nationalist politics. This separation was in the interest of state and capital, which were afraid of the unity between labour and nationalist politicians. Trade union "economism" was further deepened by the return of trade union leaders who began going for training in Britain, Europe, West Africa and the new Labour College in Kampala. These leaders had absorbed trade union economism. British and European Trade Unionism was steeped into the ideology of economism and so was the labour college at Kampala which was dominated by the International Confederation of Free Trade Unions (ICFTU), itself dominated by the U.S.A.'s AFL-CIO. The separation of trade unionism from nationalist politics was to continue to assert itself in the post-colonial era.

The relationship between the unions and the nationalist movement was however not as simple as it is made to appear. It was quite complex. While the guiding principle held by the unions was that trade unionism should be separate from nationalist politics, individual trade union leaders involved themselves in nationalist politics at various levels while advocating for the autonomy of trade unions. The mine workers for example, supported political change but were unwilling to subordinate the union to the nationalist party – the dominant one being the United National Independence Party (UNIP) which broke away from the African National Congress in 1958. The mine workers still supported UNIP even while refusing to be subordinated to it. The same trend was observed in Tanzania between the Tanzania Federation of Labour (TFL) and the Tanganyika African National Union (TANU). The former separated trade unionism from nationalist politics.[44] This division was in fact common in British Colonial Africa.

Other unions were reluctant to follow the AMWU line of separation of trade unionism from nationalist politics. There was also dissension within AMWU on this point. The leaders of the General Workers' Union and the Shop Assistants' Union for example engaged in both union activities and nationalist politics. Some of these eventually became full time activist UNIP leaders.[45] This explains the other stream of trade unionism in colonial and post-colonial Zambia – the participation of former union leaders in full time politics. The conflict between the two factions of the trade union leadership over the question of the labour movement's relationship to nationalist politics weakened the trade union movement in the late fifties and early sixties. It however did not destroy it as post-independence events would show. The conflict between the two perspectives on trade union relationship to nationalist politics led to the split in 1959 in the Trade Union Congress (TUC), which was an amalgamation of African trade unions. A Reformed Trade Union Congress (RTUC), affiliated to and active in UNIP was born. In later years, the labour movement would regard the 1959/60 split as a near split, and not as a split:

> Those who actively took part in the political struggle in Zambia will undoubtedly agree that even when political parties came on the scene, none of them could claim absolute command of membership in industrial centres without active support of trade unions. This political alliance almost tore the labour movement to pieces in 1960. However, common sense prevailed when the unified labour movement decided to support the most progressive party (UNIP).[46]

The two wings however rejoined again shortly afterwards as the United Trade Union Congress (UTUC). However, the division between trade unionism and nationalist politics was quite artificial, as was the division between the respective leaders. While some trade union leaders emerged as a result of their long service and experience in the workplace, some assumed those roles as a result of education and/or government service. In short, trade union leaders and nationalist politicians were from the same emerging class of African petty bourgeoisie, created by colonial institutions e.g. education, government service, promotion at work places etc. Their division was inspired by the colonial state and management as already stated and fostered by some self-interested union leaders who wanted to protect their turf from the intrusion of politicians. At the same time, however, these trade unionists fought against colonialism as hard as anybody else for that matter. In fact even after independence, trade unionists still boasted of having spearheaded nationalist politics.[47]

Responding for example to the constant taunting by politicians that trade unions were only for themselves and not interested in the welfare of the nation, ZCTU has countered thus:

> It must be remembered that the first people to shed blood through the bullets of the satanic colonial employers and exploiters were the workers. It is undeniable that it was through the workers' leaders who had been restricted and later banished to their home areas that active political consciousness was awakened among our people and hence the springing up of political parties. The labour movement too, morally and materially supported the political struggle right from the beginning to the end. But that does not mean they sold their will to continue fighting for industrial justice.[48]

The labour movement has put its contribution to nationalist struggle in stark political terms, which clearly has demonstrated political and class consciousness:

> In Zambia, it was the workers and their Trade Union Leaders particularly in the mining industry that stirred political consciousness among the masses because they were the first to feel the pinch of the ruthlessness of the colonizer through his political and economic exploitation even long before political parties were heard of. They organized successful civil and industrial disobedience against the colonial master...The reasons for workers quick political awareness is easy to understand. The workers realized that their chief enemy was not the company boss, but the colonial regime itself.[49]

Thus workers clearly perceived political and class relations under colonialism. The labour movement has also been conscious of what kind of trade unionism the colonial state and capital preferred, not only in Zambia, but in Africa as a whole. The colonial state and capital preferred apolitical trade unions:

The colonial authorities preferred reformist unions to the militant ones and therefore concentrated their efforts on the orientation of the trade union leaders towards this end through massive propaganda literatures and the holding of a series of seminars. The European reformist trade unions were allowed to collaborate with the African trade unions. The aim was to make African trade unions apolitical and confine them to the bread and butter issues of their members.[50]

Through engagement in strikes and so on, trade unions served as strong bases for and the driving force of the liberation struggle. The labour leaders in Zambia are also acutely conscious of the labour histories of other African countries. They have been impressed by the Nigeria General Strike of 1945, the Kenyan General Strike of 1950, the General Strike in Ghana, in 1950, the 1953 wave of strikes organized by Franco-Phone trade unions and their own strikes on the copperbelt in the 1950s.[51] Thus the labour leaders in Zambia as in all of Africa have been very cognizant of their past which the bureaucratic bourgeoisie have tried to belittle, in order to justify their repression.

Notes

1.   E. P. Thompson, *The Making of the English working class* (Harmondsworth: Penguin, 1963) p. 8.

2.   I examined Marx's framework in greater detail in a conference paper from which the following analysis is drawn. Munyonzwe Hamalengwa, "Primitive Accumulation and the Reproduction of the Rural Population: A Preliminary Comparative Framework", Paper presented at the XII*th* International Conference of the Institute for International Development and Co-operation at the University of Ottawa, October 29-31, 1981 on Rural Development and Retention of the Rural Population in the Countryside of Developing Countries. A revised version of this paper was published in french as "L'accumulation primitive et La Reproduction De La Population Rurale en Afrique" in Jose Havet, ed., *Le Village Et Le Bidonville* (Ottawa: University of Ottawa Press, 1986) pp. 79-101.

3.   Karl Marx, *Capital* Vol.1 (Moscow: Progress Publishers, 1977 edn.) p. 668.

4.   Ibid., p. 689.

5.   "The events that transformed the small peasants into wage-labourers, and their means of subsistence and of labour into material elements of capital, created, at the same time, a home market for the latter. Formerly the peasant family produced the means of subsistence and the raw materials, which they themselves, for the most part, consumed. These raw materials and means of subsistence have now become commodities; the large farmer sells them, he finds his market in manufacturers." Marx, Ibid., p. 699.

6.   V. I. Lenin; *The Development of Capitalism in Russia* (Moscow: Progress Publishers, 1977 edn.) Chapter VIII.

7.   See Harold Wolpe, "Capitalism and Cheap Labour-power in South Africa: From Segregation to Apartheid" *Economy And Society* 1, No.4 1972, pp. 425-56 and Martin Legassick, "Legislation, Ideology and Economy in Post-1948 South Africa" *Journal of Southern African Studies* 1, No.1 1974, pp. 5-35 and "South Africa: Capital Accumulation and Violence" *Economy and Society* 3, No.3 1974, pp. 253-91.

8.   Govan Arrighi, "Labour Supplies in Historical Perspective: A Study of the Proletarianization of the African Peasantry in Rhodesia" in Giovanni Arrighi and John S. Saul, *Essays on The Political Economy of Africa* (New York and London: Monthly Review Press, 1973).

9.   Christopher Leo, *Land and Class in Kenya*, (Toronto: University of Toronto Press, 1984).

10.   For a Comprehensive and Sophisticated Analysis, see Lionel Cliffe, "Rural Political Economy of Africa", in: *The Political Economy of Contemporary Africa* (Beverly Hills and London: Sage Publications, 1976) Edited by Peter C. W. Gutkind and Immanuel Wallerstein, pp. 112-131.

11. Quoted in John S. Saul and Stephen Gelb "The Crisis in South Africa: Class Defense, Class Revolution" *Monthly Review* Vol.33 No.3 Special Issue (July-August) 1981, p. 92.

12. Joel Samoff, "Underdevelopment and its Grass Roots in Africa" *Canadian Journal of African Studies* Vol. 14 No.1, 1980, pp. 5-36.

13. For the most comprehensive case study of this situation, see, Issa G. Shivji, *Law, State and the Working Class in Tanzania* (London: James Currey, 1986).

14. For good historical works on this period and after, see, L. H. Gann, *The Birth of A Plural Society: The Development of Northern Rhodesia Under the British South* Africa Company (Manchester: Manchester University Press, 1958). Michael Gelfand, *Northern Rhodesia in The Days of The Charter* (Oxford: Basil Blackwell, 1961), and L. H. Gann, *A History of Northern Rhodesia: Early Days to 1953* (London: Chatto and Windus, 1964).

15. Quoted in F. L. Coleman, *The Northern Rhodesia Copperbelt 1889-1962* (Manchester: Manchester University Press, 1971) p. 2.

16. Reproduced as Appendix 11, "Land and Mineral Concessions", in L. H. Gann, *The Birth of A Plural Society* note 14, p. 216.

17. Jane Parpart, *Labour and Capital on the African Copperbelt* (Philadelphia: Temple University Press, 1984) p. 16.

18. For comprehensive introductory works on colonial land policies, see, Frances Carpenter, "The Introduction of Commercial Farming into Zambia and its Effects, to 1940" pp. 1-14, and Robin Palmer, "Land in Zambia" pp. 56-66 both in Robin Palmer (ed.) *Zambian Land and Labour Studies* Vol.1 (Lusaka: National Archives of Zambia Occasional Paper No.2, 1973). For a case study of the making of a peasantry, see, Kenneth Powers Vickery, *The Making of A Peasantry: Imperialism and The Tonga Plateau Economy 1890-1936*, Ph.D. Thesis, Yale University, 1978. For the land question in Central and Southern Africa, see, Robin Palmer and Neil Parsons (eds.), *The Roots of Rural Poverty in Central and Southern Africa* (Berkeley: University of California Press, 1977).

19. Carpenter, Ibid., p. 6.

20. Gelfand, note 14, p. 147.

21. L. H. Gann, *The Birth of A Plural Society*, note 14, Quoted in Richard Sklar, *Corporate Power in An African State: The Political Impact of Multinational Mining Companies in Zambia* (Berkeley et al.: University of California Press, 1975) p. 98.

22. See, Sklar, Ibid., p. 98-99.

23. Issa Shivji, note 13.

24. Helmuth Heisler, "A Class of Target-Proletarians", *Journal of Asian and African Studies* 5 (July 1970) pp. 161-175, Quoted in Sklar, note 21, p. 99.

25. Sklar, Ibid.

26. For a fuller study of the proletarianization occasioned by the copper industry, see, Elena L. Berger, *Labour, Race and Colonial Rule: The Copperbelt from 1924 to Independence* (Oxford: Clarendon Press, 1974). Complementary studies include, Philip Daniel, *Africanization, Nationalization and Inequality: Mining Labour and the Copperbelt in Zambian Development* (Cambridge: Cambridge University Press, 1979) and Jane Parpart, note 17.

27. Marx *Capital* Vol.1, note 3, p. 600. This analysis is borrowed from my earlier work, see note 2.

28. Ibid., p. 601.

29. Ibid., p. 602.

30. Parpart, note 17, p. 23.

31. For a refutation of this deliberate policy, see, A. L. Epstein, *Politics in An Urban Community* (Manchester: Manchester University Press, 1958).

32. See Berger, note 26.

33. For a summary of the imposition of English law into Zambia, see my study, "The Legal System of Zambia: Colonial Origins and Contemporary Perspectives" paper presented at the 13th World Congress on Philosophy of Law and Social Philosophy, at Kobe, Japan, August 20-26, 1987, forthcoming in the proceedings of the Congress.

34. For studies of these strikes, see, Ian Henderson, "Early African Leadership: The Copperbelt Disturbances of 1935 and 1940" *Journal of Southern African Studies*, No.2, 1975, pp. 83-97; Charles Perrings, "Consciousness, Conflict and Proletarianization: An Assessment of the 1935 Mineworkers' Strike on the Northern Rhodesian Copperbelt" *Journal of Southern African Studies*, No.4, 1977, pp. 31-51, and Michael Murphy, "The 1935 Copperbelt Disturbances Commission: A Critical Assessment" in Robin Palmer (ed.) *Zambian Land and Labour Studies*, note 18, pp. 32-40.

35. *Report of the Commission Appointed to Inquire into the Disturbances on the Copperbelt of Northern Rhodesia* (The Russel Commission), (Md. 5009 (HMSO, London 1935) see also *Evidence taken by the Commission Appointed to Inquire into the Disturbances on the Copperbelt of Northern Rhodesia, July to September 1935* (Lusaka: Government Printer, 1935).

36. Translated by an African Clerk who was present at the scene, Quoted in Wilson Chakulya, *Zambia and the International Labour Organization* (Lusaka: Government Printer, 1969) p. 20.

37. The Russel Report, note 35, p. 26 and W. Richard Jacobs, "The Relationship Between the African Trade Unions and Political Organizations in Northern Rhodesia/Zambia, 1949-1961" (Geneva: International Institute for Labour Studies paper, 1971) p. 1.

38. Perrings, note 34, Parpart, note 17.

39. *Report of the Commission Appointed to Inquire into the Disturbances in the Copperbelt of Northern Rhodesia* (Forster Report) (Lusaka: Government Printer, 1940) see also Jacobs, note 37, p. 2.

40. Forster Report, Ibid., p. 25 and Jacobs, Ibid., p. 2.

41. Jacobs, Ibid., p. 2.

42. For a concise description of these relationships, see Jacobs, note 37.

43. For a review of these developments, see Parpart, note 17.

44. See Shivji, note 13.

45 See description in Chakulya, note 36 and Jacobs, note 37.

46. *Workers Voice*, Vol.3 No.3 (October 1980) p. 9.

47 See, the pages of *Workers Voice*, the official publication of the Zambia Congress of Trade Unions (ZCTU).

48 The *Workers Voice*, Vol.3 No.3 (October 1980) p. 6.

49. Ibid., p. 9.

50. "Unions and Politics" in *Workers Voice*, Vol.3 No.2 (September 1980) p. 8.

51. Ibid.

52. Ibid.

4

The Growth of the State Bourgeoisie in Zambia

In the previous chapter, I detailed the growth of the Zambian working class. In this chapter I discuss briefly and in the abstract the origins of the indigenous class that took over the reigns of state power at independence in 1964 and how it used that state position to entrench itself politically and economically in the following years. This will set the stage for further discussion of the relationship between this state bourgeoisie and the working classes, which relationship I will characterise as premised on class struggles.

I should forewarn the reader here that I will not be discussing the state bourgeoisie empirically – I have not done empirical research yet, but will discuss this class in terms of its general policies, practices of accumulation using its position in the state and its policies towards the working class. In other words, I will not be mentioning names of individuals and what property they have accumulated using their position in the state. I can only state that there are observable tendencies that Zambia's ruling class can be seen as a class of enrichers in Fanon's sense and some of its members have transformed themselves into proper capitalists after having used the state as the principal vehicle of accumulation.[1]

The historical origins of the African ruling class in general can be traced to the traditional ruling classes (kings, chiefs etc.), land owners, merchants, traders and religious leaders.[2] The future leaders, the majority of whom had a head start by being born in one of these families, had to be channelled through the education process. Some passed through the military barracks as is now quite evident. Education was the common denominator.

In the case of Zambia, most of the first generation independence leaders, the majority of whom are still in power, education was the vehicle that propelled them into leadership positions, of course after having had a head start because of their family backgrounds. Thus the insistence on class analysis is quite cogent. Kenneth Kaunda, a former teacher is the son of a religious leader; Mainza Chona (the first Zambian lawyer) and others are sons of chiefs; the first African National Congress (ANC) leader, Lewanika was from the Lozi Royal Family; Simon Kapwepwe and many others were highly educated at the time etc. etc.; others made it through the trade union route. Hardly any of the leaders was bourgeois proper, in terms of owning independent means of production – either industrial, commercial, landed or agrarian. They also neither belonged to the traditional middle class, they could only be character-ized as "educated middle class".[3] They were pretty much like their Tanzanian counterparts.[4] At times though, conflict has developed between the less edu-cated and more educated of these "educated middle class." Anti-intellectualism has sometimes reared its head in Zambian politics.

Like in most African countries, the Zambian independence struggle was waged along populist rather than class lines. The contradiction was seen as between imperialism (foreign occupation) and the African people. The struggle was seen as aimed at supplanting imperialism. Once this was achieved, it was assumed everything would be okay. But this was not to be.

At independence of Zambia in 1964, those who assumed political office were immediately saddled with continuous pressures from four sources:

1.   massive repatriation of profits by multinational corporations

2.   massive demand for wage increases by African workers, especially on the copperbelt

3.   glaring rural poverty demanding massive injection of money, and

4.   pressure from within and without the main political party for eco-nomic and political aggrandizement.

Each of these pressures as well as political and economic pressures emanating from the South-Rhodesia, Portuguese colonies of Angola and Mo-zambique, South Africa and Namibia had to be addressed urgently. How some of these problems were dealt with will be the subject of the following chapters. Stated briefly the repatriation of profits was partly solved by nationalization and joint ownership of major economic enterprises; wage demands were solved somewhat haphazardly by pluralism in industrial relations and repression and it has been the subject of continuing class struggles; rural poverty was the subject of numerous half-hearted attempts at resolution and political pressures were partly dealt with by economic reforms, the introduction of the one-party state system, repression and other methods.

Despite all these pressures those holding state power never veered from using state power to enrich themselves. Baylies and Szeftel who perhaps have done more empirical study than anybody else, in the area of *embourgeoisement* of the Zambian political class and enrichment of local capital, state the following:

> If small, the new bourgeoisie – and to a lesser extent the whole emerging indigenous capitalist class – enjoyed a strategic affinity with the state and the state elite. Indeed, at the upper echelons of the owning class the state elite could be said to be a significant "class of recruitment" for the new bourgeoisie. Those members of the owning class entering large scale capitalist operations in commerce, transport, engineering and manufacturing, or combining a number of such interests, tended to be drawn disproportionately from the ranks of professionals and from the top layers of the party, civil service and parastatals. Among African holding state land around Lusaka in the early seventies, forty-eight (or thirty-two percent) either had been or still were involved in the top levels of the party, the parastatals and the civil service. And of the 91 people who could be characterised as a true bourgeoisie, at least thirty-six percent had held or continued to hold positions in the upper levels of the party, government or public enterprises.[5]

Note that this was in the early seventies. Now the state personnel who double as collective as well as private capitalists are many more in number and most likely are richer capitalists. Of course to mask their holdings, some probably use their children or wives or husbands as fronts. This would be a useful area of empirical research – to uncover the nature and extent of *embourgeoisement* of the Zambian ruling class. These same people would not hesitate to use the power of the state to protect their interests against the working class.

In his 1987 edition of *Humanism in Zambia and a Guide to Its Implementation*, Kaunda reiterates his perception of growing *embourgeoisement* and entrenchment of the capitalist class in Zambia since the first economic reforms of 1968: "During this period we have witnessed, perhaps, the unconscious growth of classes; an unexpected consequence of the well-meant economic reforms. We have witnessed, too, the beginning of what should be this society's people's wealth, becoming entrenched in the hands of a few."[6] Kaunda nowhere identifies the make-up of this "powerful Zambian elite"[7] and why it was allowed to develop in the face of the Leadership Code. There is failure to recognise that the political class is part of this powerful Zambian economic elite. With this blindness, it is not surprising that a powerful indigenous class can grow unchecked. Even those in the political leadership who have remained honest, the state supplies so many free goods that they may as well not accumulate on their own. So long as they did not fall out of favour with the system, they could live comfortably forever. A slogan even developed "UNIP pays."

The truth of the matter is that one of the aims of the economic reforms which started in 1968 was to encourage the development of indigenous capital. That indigenous capital did grow was a necessary result. That the political class would enrich itself was also a necessary result.

One of the other aims was to reduce the overwhelming influence of foreign capital and to encourage a mixed type of economy – private and public ownership of the means of production. The politics and rationale of mixed economies has been theorised quite often. Scholars have identified three different radical perspectives on mixed economies in advanced capitalist countries which may have application to the Zambian situation:[8]

1.   that state enterprise is an instrument with which a unified and far-sighted capitalist class furthers its own special interests;

2.   that state enterprise is a means by which a relatively autonomous state seeks to fulfill the needs of a divided, myopic group of capitalists; and

3.   state enterprise is a tool of a class coalition between workers and capitalists.

Freeman calls the first school as the instrumental school and represented by Miliband and O'Connor, the second as the functionalist school and represented by the German capital school one of whose proponents is Claus Offe and the third as the class compromise school represented by Wallerstein and Przeworski.

The instrumentalists hold according to Freeman that government commercial activity serves only the interests of the capitalist class. State enterprise is merely one of several means capitalists use to achieve their ends. In the case of Zambia, I think it is more correct to state that the mixed or joint enterprises were aimed at reducing the influence of multinational corporations in order to enhance the interests of the political class as well as indigenous capital. The capitalist class whose interests were to be served were not external to the state class per se. The state was to be deeply enmeshed in economic management and not merely to superintend on behalf of the capitalist class. International capital in fact was initially alarmed at the takeover but immediately adjusted and continued to reap the benefits. However, room was opened for indigenous accumulation including that of the political class. The above observations also answer the functionalist accounts of mixed economies.

The functionalists according to Freeman, argue that the key to understanding the politics of mixed economies lies in the "objective relation" between the state and the capitalist class, specifically the way the state stabilizes and reproduces the capitalist system of production. They maintain that the mix of private and public enterprise is not a tool of an all powerful capitalist class but rather a functional requisite of capitalism, discovered and enforced by a relatively autonomous state. The state realises that the capitalist economic activity cannot be sustained and the class struggle cannot be effectively managed unless publicly-owned business ventures are undertaken. It therefore builds a societal consensus for erecting a mixed economy.

This view when applied to Zambia is correct in so far as it recognizes that joint enterprises could have the effect of managing class struggle between labour and capital. If Labour is convinced that joint management is both for the interests of workers and the whole country, they may tamper their militancy. This seems to have been attempted in Zambia. It will be shown later that labour was not convinced that nationalization of the mines and other enterprises necessarily benefitted workers.

The class compromise school holds that mixed economies are embarked upon to uphold or enforce a class compromise between classes. Both the capitalist class and the workers need the interposition of the state. In the case of Zambia, I am urging that the state embarked on this project to entrench the economic and political position of the political class as against those of multinational capital, it was not to cement any class compromise between labour and capital. Of course the project was sold as benefiting the workers though the workers did not buy this smokescreen.

In the following chapters, I detail how the collective state capitalist class went about trying to entrench their economic and political power and how the working classes conducted their class struggles for a share of the economic pie.

Notes

1. I am paraphrasing Susanne Mueller's article on Tanzania, "The Historical Origins of Tanzania's Ruling Class" *Canadian Journal of African Studies* Vol. 15, No. 3, 1981 p. 462.

2. See, "The State and the Crisis in Africa: In Search of a Second Liberation" *Development Dialogue* No. 2, 1987 p. 14.

3. Ibid.

4. See Mueller, note 1.

5. Carolyn Baylies and Morris Szeftel, "The rise of a Zambian Capitalist Class in the 1970s" *Journal of Southern African Studies* Vol. 8, No. 2, 1982 pp. 195-6.

6. Lusaka: Kenneth Kaunda Foundation, 1987 p. 127.

7. Ibid.

8. See Freeman, *The Politics of Mixed Economies*, Ithaca: Cornell University Press, forthcoming.

5

Class Struggles in Zambia, Phase 1, 1964 – 1971

▮▮ The Zambian State apparatus to an apparently large degree function[ed] as a source for exploitation by the bureaucratic bourgeoisie and as a means of redistributing income which properly belongs with the majority of the population to this office-holding sectional interest".[1] This exploitation and embourgeoisement by the state or bureaucratic bourgeoisie takes many forms and guises and as editorialised by the *Times of Zambia* these include "scandalous business transactions, malpractices, fraudulent accounting, financial mismanagement – the list is endless and almost as nauseating".[2]

The state acquired majority ownership of foreign firms in all sectors of the economy and a number of conglomerates were established to control the operation of these various undertakings: the Zambia Industrial and Mining Corporation (ZIMCO) was created as the umbrella body, one of the largest conglomerates in Africa – which controlled the Industrial Development Corporation (INDECO), which administered the government's industrial and commercial interests, while Mining Development Corporation (MINDECO) acted in a similar manner towards the state's mining ventures, and Financial Development Corporation (FINDECO) for the financial institutions, also under ZIMCO's overall direction. It is in these state parastatal institutions that the parastatal fraction of the state bourgeoisie blossomed. And this state controlled economic sector served the interests of the whole bureaucratic bourgeoisie. It was their avenue for capital accumulation.

The state and government-based fraction of the bureaucratic bourgeoisie was also blossoming as a result of their control of the state resources accruing from state control of the economy, from high salaries, free housing, free cars, easy access to loans; from corruption and robbery etc. The high military, security and police officers also shared in this embourgeoisement by being appointed to head government institutions and sharing in the privileges.

The economic reforms of 1968[3], 1969[4] and later[5] made the state the largest employer in the country. By 1982, the state was controlling 70% to 80% of economic activity in Zambia.[6]

The nationalizations and economic reforms of 1968 and 1969 were an act of economic nationalism, an act of struggle between the bureaucratic bourgeoisie on the one hand and international capital and foreign resident bourgeoisie on the other hand. The state bourgeoisie perceived that international and foreign resident bourgeoisies were not faithful to the economic interests of Zambia, leaving the former vulnerable economically. Thus to be financially autonomous, nationalizations and other reforms became necessary. At the 1968 conference of UNIP at Mulungushi, Kaunda declared it unacceptable that the Zambian economy should continue to be directed by foreign companies.

Kaunda criticized the mining companies and other foreign controlled companies for their gross under-capitalization, excessive local borrowing, and intolerably high level of dividend remittances.[7] Dividend remittance by the mining companies was simply naked economic exploitation as Table 5.1 shows for the Roan Selection Trust Group.

Table 5.1

**Net Profit and Dividend Distribution of
Roan Selection Trust, 1960-67**

Year	Net Profit Km	Retained in Business – Km	Dividends Km
1960	9.4	5.1	4.2
1961	6.6	3.5	3.2
1962	11.2	2.6	8.6
1963	11.9	2.3	9.5
1964	11.8	2.2	9.5
1965	17.4	3.9	13.5
1966	20.5	3.1	15.3
1967	20.7	5.3	15.4

Source: Introduction to the *Mulungushi Declaration*

It can seen that the net profit rose significantly from the early sixties and jumped geometrically after independence. The proportion of repatriated dividends over what was retained in the business also rose significantly. On 11th August 1969, during UNIP's National Council meeting at Matero Hall in Lusaka, Kaunda struck at the Mining companies:

> I shall ask the owners of the mines to invite the government to join their mining enterprises. I am asking the owners of the mines to give 51 percent of their shares to the State.

It is not necessary here to do a detailed account of the success or failure of these nationalizations. This has been ably done by others[8] serve to say that the nationalizations irrevocably ushered in a new class of Zambians whose fate was tied to these mining companies and parastatal institutions.

The leading spokespeople of the bureaucratic bourgeoisie while aware of the class forming in the interstices of the state and the exploitation by this class, stirred the problem of class exploitation in another direction – the cleavage between the urban and rural areas. Class formation in the state was relegated to the question of the problem of "class consciousness". Addressing a rally on International Literacy Day on September 8, 1968, President Kaunda lamented, "already, as a result of the differences in our educational accomplishment, one can see the beginning of a class consciousness... In the majority of cases, the educated members of our society also happened to be the junior members, and through the good fortune of having had the advantage of a sound education those young men and women are daily being thrust into responsible public positions and offices of trust [in government]... In its extreme form, government by a select group of men leads to exploitation of majority and because of their continued exclusion from the affairs of the nation, the general public tends to withdraw from any direct involvement in the running of their government and those in power take this opportunity to entrench their position".[9]

Even with this perception, Kaunda did not see a problem of class exploitation and class antagonism in the urban areas. It was not like in capitalist economies. "Capitalist economies have been described as creating two nations within one – the bourgeoisie and the proletariat; that is, the property owners on the one hand and on the other, the industrial and farm workers who lack their own means of production and hence sell the labour to live-in simple language, the rich and the poor... Here in Zambia we also face the danger of creating two nations within one. But not along the capitalist pattern. The important division in our society is not that which exists between trade union labour on the one hand and managers and property owners on the other, but between the urban and rural areas. These are the two nations we are running the danger of creating; these are the two parts of our dualism; urban and rural and not so much between labour and employers".[10] Kaunda further observed that the average income of Zambians in paid employment was already about K750 per annum which was about eight times the income of the subsistence farmer, representing a greater gap than that between the urban Zambian and the expatriate. This interpretation of data by Kaunda seems to be a variant of the labour aristocracy thesis i.e. workers are more well off than the other citizens, in this case peasants.

After this blurring of class relations in the urban Milieu in favour of ventilating the question of the rural-urban gap, Kaunda went on to deliver his central message, a tirade against workers; "I have said that class consciousness is one of the biggest dangers in Zambia. Workers can themselves be a source of force in the creation of classes. By trying to group themselves together and distinguish themselves from the rest of society in pursuit of what they may believe to be their own interests as workers, they provoke response from the rest of their fellow men, who naturally organize themselves to protect their own interests in turn. For Zambia, it is ridiculous for workers now in the light of these (economic) reforms to feel that they are a distinct class pursuing distinct interests. No, the interests of factory workers, road and other manual workers, the teachers, the civil servants, the police, the armed forces, any type of workers, indeed politicians, are all identical".[11] This was tantamount to saying that there were no distinct classes and hence no distinct class interests in Zambia. Since the state controlled the major means of production, the state being the trustee of the whole people of Zambia, all the benefits would accrue to the whole people. "Thus for a [trade] union to push a claim against the state is to push a claim against the people".[12] This is a variant of the unitary model of industrial relations which does not acknowledge any divergence of interests between managers and workers or between capital and labour.

This was the ideological justification the state-based section of the Zambian bourgeoisie i.e. the bureaucratic bourgeoisie used to try to control the working class in Zambia. This was a tactic of its class struggle against the working class. The working class was seen as promoting sectional interests rather than promoting general interests i.e. public interest of society.[13] The state, as per the bureaucratic bourgeoisie controlling the state, was there to promote not sectional interests but interests of the society as a whole. Sectional interests were subordinated to societal interests. The public interest put forward frequently was that of the need for rapid economic development.[14] This chapter discusses the various class struggles between the bureaucratic bourgeoisie and the working class between 1964 and 1971.

The state pursued a variety of ways to try to control the working class: ideological-part of what has been said above; legislation and organizational – the creation of the Zambia Congress of Trade Unions (ZCTU) in 1965 and the appointment of top ranking persons of this federation of unions by the state, and, repression. We consider the last two in turn.

It has already been mentioned that during the colonial era, African trade unions deliberately decided to form one federation of unions – the Northern Rhodesia Trade Union Congress. This was a voluntary act by trade unionists themselves, whose aim was to unite for the promotion and defence of African working class interests. Of course there were conflicts, frictions and splits in the TUC but there were no externally imposed conditions or manipulations as to who the president or other office bearers in the union should be.

This position was changed swiftly after independence. One of the major acts the new state undertook immediately after independence was to legislate a new federation of trade unions in Zambia. The Trade Unions and Trade Disputes (Amendment) Act (of 1965) was passed which among other concerns created the Zambia Congress of Trade Unions. Needless to say this Act was intended to extend government control over trade union officials and hence the labour movement as a whole, by restricting the field from which union leadership might be drawn, prohibiting any affiliation with or financial assistance from outside bodies without ministerial permission etc. These developments may have led to the result that ZCTU trade union leadership was highly mistrusted by affiliated unions during the first few years of independence.[15] Labour leaders were appointed by the state.

We call this tactic of trying to control the working class by forming a federation of unions whose leadership may be manipulated by the state, an attempt at imposing organizational hegemony[16] i.e. trying to reorganize the working class so as to best control it. Organizational hegemony is just one of the tactics the bureaucratic bourgeoisie used to wage their class struggle against the working class.

The ZCTU was registered in 1966 with affiliated unions numbering 12. Table 5.2 shows the membership of some of the affiliated unions in 1968.

The unions affiliated to the ZCTU were required by legislation to subscribe to certain prescribed decisions; which were to have ZCTU approval before implementation by any union:

1.   to hold a strike ballot or call a strike;

2.   to dissolve a trade union;

3.   to reconstitute a trade union as two or more unions;

4.   to amalgamate with one or more trade unions;

5.   to affiliate to a federation of trade unions;

Table 5.2

Federation of Trade Unions

	Year of Registration	Membership at
Zambia Congress of Trade Unions	1966	31-12-68
The Affiliated Trade Unions were:		
Mine Workers' Union of Zambia (Amalgamated in 1967)	1967	46,096
National Union of Building, Engineering and General Workers	1960	15.000
National Union of Commercial and Industrial Workers	1960	11,000
National Union of Public Service Workers	1960	10,000
National Union of Local Authorities Workers	1961	8,888
Zambia Railways Amalgamated Workers Union (Amalgamated in 1967)	1967	6,018
National Union of Plantation and Agricultural Workers	1962	5,100
National Union of Postal and Telecommunications Workers	1964	1,532
Hotel Catering Workers Union of Zambia	1966	1,435
Zambia Typographical Union	1961	919

Source: *Annual Report of the Department of Labour*, 1968
Government Printer, Lusaka, p. 59.

6.   to impose a levy;

7.   to increase or decrease the subscription or entrance fees of members; and

8.   to alter or amend the rules of trade union or to change its organizational structure.

Further the law now required that to qualify for election as an officer of a trade union a person must have worked for three years in the particular occupation or industry with which the union is directly concerned. If the union had less than 500 members an official was to be actually employed in the industry. We will evaluate below whether this attempt at organizational hegemony was successful in achieving its aims.

Regarding state repressive measures, Zambia inherited a formidable instrument for the control of "unruly" elements or unwelcome developments -- emergency powers (EPS). Emergency powers were extensively used during the colonial era to control the working class and nationalist politicians. By *Emergency Powers Act, 1964* the newly independent Zambia continued with emergency powers and by *Constitution (Amendment) Act, 1969*, emergency powers were entrenched to be applicable indefinitely. I regard them as one of the arsenals available to the state bourgeoisie with which it waged its class struggles. Arrest and detentions were the main tactics used under emergency powers. It will be seen below how these emergency powers were used against the working class in Zambia.

Working Class Struggles

Most of the issues the African working class were fighting for during the colonial era were unresolved at independence in 1964. Such was the issue involving pay scales whereby Europeans were paid many more times than Africans, and such was the case involving African advancement in general. Investigating the pay structures in the civil service in 1963 for example, the Hadow commission found four separate pay scales within the civil service, differing according to the race or the date of employment of the civil servant. This was after a non-racial civil service had supposedly been in existence since 1961. The Hadow commission produced a unified civil service pay structure.[17]

On the mines however, the pay rise that the mineworkers demanded at independence was tied to their accepting a dual wage structure. European workers were to continue to be paid more. The miners decided to accept a pay rise as the price for accepting a dual wage structure. This meant a postponement of the struggle for a uniform wage structure to another date for the miners. This situation also later caused friction within the mineworkers union itself.

At independence the African workers expected the new government to favourably respond to their interests – African advancement, which meant promotion to European-held jobs and hefty wage increases or at least a uniform pay scale with the European workers. But as pointed out earlier the new government thought the African urban workers were already highly paid enough, in fact many times more than their rural brethren. Thus the new state and the African working class were on a collision course right from the beginning.

In January 1966, the African mineworkers went on a strike over racial pay disparities. The government had not yet come up with a wage and salary policy even though it was a major issue with the workers. In response to the strike, the government appointed a commission of inquiry under the chairmanship of Roland Brown to examine the disparities between the expatriate and local conditions of service. The Zambia Mineworkers Union did not like the appointment of Roland Brown. It was the same Brown who had recommended the abolition of trade unions and the lowering of wages in Tanzania. They did not want the same thing to happen in Zambia. They preferred a local person. The miners also did not appreciate not having been informed officially of the impending commission. They were also surprised that the Secretary-General of ZCTU, Augustine Nkumbula was to be a commissioner, instead of representing trade unions. No wonder the unions were suspicious of ZCTU during this time. Nevertheless after assurances from the government that a foreign chairman would be more objective than a local person or somebody from mine headquarters in London, the commission went ahead. In its report, the Brown Commission recommended establishing a single basic pay scale, with expatriate allowances for foreign workers. The commission found it difficult to decide what factors should determine the basic pay scale.

The existing expatriate pay scale was rejected as a basis because, *(a)* it would be excessively inflationary, *(b)* it was based on an inappropriate notion of privilege, being fixed sufficiently high to secure a 'European way of life' for those on that pay scale, and, *(c)* because the effect of collective bargaining in the past had been to introduce widespread anomalies into the scale. The former local scale was also unacceptable as a basis because it deliberately undervalued the skills of African workers. It had been built from established points on the scale of African wages by a process of job evaluation, without reference to European rates from the same or similar work. The European miners were able to secure for themselves high wages because industrial skill in Zambia was scarce. It was still scarce and would remain so for many years to come. Its value to the employer did not depend on race or colour, but by isolating African wages from any connection with European wages the mining companies appeared to have devalued the skill which the Africans could acquire now for the first time.[18]

The commission recommended a 22 percent wage increase to be applied uniformly throughout the former African scale, justifying this big award in terms of the need to do something significant if there was to be any chance of industrial peace in the mining industry. With the unification of pay scales in the mining sector, the rest of the sectors could follow suit.

The disparity between African and European wages was not the only disparity in wages in Zambia. There were wage disparities between urban and rural incomes, between sectors e.g. mining and manufacturing, between skilled and unskilled workers and between lower and higher civil service salaries etc. To look into these wage disparities, the government appointed the Whelan Civil Service Salaries Commission,[19] shortly after the Brown Commission. The Whelan Commission proposed a graduated wage awards whereby the lowest paid would receive a 25 percent increase down to 15 percent for the highest paid. The commission also proposed ending differentials between rural and urban civil services pay scales, which was followed by other sectors. Wage increases for all sectors thus resulted from unification and raising of pay scales. The working class was thus making impressive gains through their struggles up to 1967.

The honeymoon of wage increases ended in 1967. This can be gleaned from Table 5.4. The government realized that the pace of wage increases was too fast and the awards too high. The Local Authority Workers had to go on strike to protest the reduction from K32 to K28.17 of their pay award per month by the government. They were suppressed. The Local Authority Workers persisted with some sporadic strikes in 1968. That year also saw strikes by Railway Workers in support of a pay claim.

In anticipation of the next Mineworkers pay award, the government announced the establishment of a Salaries Commission to review civil service salaries in March 1969. An official incomes policy was also crystallizing to anticipate and restrain the next round of large wage increases. Professor H. A. Turner an I.L.O. expert was asked to prepare the ground for such a policy. But without waiting for the report, President Kaunda ordered a temporary wage freeze and a ban on "unofficial" strikes.[20] As if there was prior agreement between Kaunda and Turner, the latter blamed higher wages without correspondingly higher labour productivity for Zambia's unprecedented rate of inflation after 1966 and for the marked slowdown in employment creation. Turner recommended a system of wage and price controls.[21] Thus Turner and the Zambian state were at one in condemning the higher wages and the perceived low productivity of the working class in Zambia. The Second National Convention of UNIP held in December 1969 applauded Turner's findings. At this Convention Kaunda announced and it was approved that wage increases would henceforth be limited to 5 percent per annum. A war against the working class was being declared.

Table 5.4

Man-Days Lost Through Strikes and Growth of Earnings

Year	% Growth in Average African Earnings over Previous Year	Man-Days of Work Lost through Strikes
1961	5.9	19,640
1962	4.9	541,894
1963	6.0	409,559
1964	19.4	125,738
1965	12.0	22,493
1966	12.1	579,406
1967	38.7	46,088
1968	7.1	65,898
1969	5.8	21,069
1970	23.1	122,951
1971	11.3	18,894
1972	-1.7	20,874
1973	11.9	5,663
1974	-1.1	38,650
1975	1.6	51,007
1976	N.A.	6,527

Source: James Fry, *Employment and Income Distribution in the African Economy*, pp. 99-100.

The 5 percent limit on wage increases caught the Railway Workers at the wrong time. They had been awarded an K8 per month increase which was about to be implemented. The K8 would have constituted more than 5 percent limit per annum. The state intervened to reduce the award. The Railway Workers had to embark on a massive strike in 1970 to claim this pay increase. A compromise was reached as a result of the strike, to divide the award into two annual increases of K4 so as to remain within the policy guidelines.[22] The strikes by the Railway Workers and the Teachers Union (discussed below) were responsible for the significant number of Man-days lost to strikes in 1970, compared to the 1967-69 and 1971-76 periods.

The series of strikes initiated by the Zambia National Union of Teachers (ZNUT) in 1970 to protest against the delay in the implementation of new conditions of service were greeted differently and harshly by the state. On 30th July 1970, 6 days after the strike was over, the President detained 4 ZNUT leaders, explaining thus:

> They sought to turn the union into an instrument for furthering the interests of organisations whose objectives are subversive. It was treacherous to deliberately seek to mislead the public such as the four teachers had been doing in the past. This does not serve the cause of Zambia, it serves the cause of enemies within our midst. The greatest enemy in this country is not an outsider but a Zambian himself who enables outsiders to succeed in the destruction of the nation.[23]

It is clear the president was pushing political motivations on the Union to justify his action. However, the dispute that led the teachers to strike had been of long standing, going back to 1968.[24] They had been waiting for two years for their recommended improved conditions of service and salaries to materialize. The Ministry of Education had all along been stalling.[25] There did not seem to be any political motivations whatsoever, serve for the politically volatile period within the ruling party at the time the strike occurred. In this respect the strike could have been used politically since as Ackson Kanduza put it, "strikes do not have to be politically motivated to be used by politicians".[26] But this period need not detain us here, as it will be discussed in Chapter 10.

An interesting development for us regarding this strike is the strong support the strikers received both from the Teachers' Union and the ZCTU. Generally up to this time the leadership of ZCTU was held at arms length by other affiliated unions, for example the MUZ and rank and file. Further since unions were generally regarded as "soft" by the general membership, it turned out that this time the national union-ZCTU, and the leadership of the union whose members were on strike-ZNUT, both supported the strike. This then must caution against wholesale condemnation of union leadership. It appears that it is important that conditions under which a union will support or distance itself from strike action should be sought out as each response is recorded. In the case of the ZNUT strike of 1970, the grievances of the members seem to have been justified and strike action was thus a necessary course of action.[27]

The fate that had greeted the ZNUT leaders also befell the leaders of the miners in May 1971 who were campaigning for a strike in opposition to the dubious pay award of 1970. The awards which resulted from a complex grading system that was agreed upon between the mines and MUZ in 1969 gave average wage increases of 10 percent to some workers and nothing to all those that were downgraded. About 1,000 workers were downgraded.[28] It was in opposition to the 1970 award that some miners began to organize for strike. In May 1971, notices appeared in several mine townships calling for an "unofficial" strike action. The state reacted firmly, as it had done earlier with the teachers, and before any strikes could occur, arrested 100 "dissident" miners and later detained 15 of their leaders.[29]

The State had thus abandoned its hands-off approach to the strikers as it had done almost continuously since 1964. Repression was taking over. This probably signalled a failure of government appeasement to the working class and authoritarianism appeared to be the answer. And it proved effective, for when the ZNUT leaders were detained in 1970, the antagonism ended and when the state detained the 15 miners in 1971, the strike did not take place.

The state also meddled in union elections to influence their outcome. In the 1966 mineworkers' election, the state sponsored its own candidates. It clearly wanted a pliable union. However, the state-sponsored candidates lost massively, prompting a UNIP regional official to say that from then onwards, the mineworkers would be regarded as an opposition to government. In 1970 the state again intervened by siding with one section of the trade union leadership in MUZ by appointing one critical trade unionist as governor and at ZCTU level it coopted the general secretary, already a government supporter, into cabinet where he soon found himself Minister of Labour and Social Services. A Minister of Labour is a crucial person in labour relations in Zambia, as anywhere. Again in 1974 the state intervened in MUZ elections by detaining some of the "dissident" leaders that had emerged in the 1970 and 1971 crises and who wanted to campaign against the incumbent leadership. Thus the state placed itself squarely on the side of the incumbent leadership. And it was not a coincidence that wage awards always came shortly before MUZ elections, possibly to ensure that the incumbent leadership was re-elected.

The pattern that emerged during the first ten years of Independence or so was that after every pay increase which generally followed major strikes (1966 and 1970) there was relative quiet in working class struggles. In between, the state set up various commissions to look into wages, salaries and incomes policies. No clear policy in any of these areas emerged. The 5 percent annum wage ceiling the state imposed in 1969 never held. The following year (1970) miners who were spearheading wage claims received on the average a 10 percent hike. Thus the 5 percent ceiling never became an incomes policy. The miners pushed their wage demands and got a 20 percent award in late 1973.

The miners did not even have to threaten to strike. The O'Riodan Salaries Commission on public service had recommended a 15-20 percent increase in 1971.[30] The Mwanakatwe Salaries Commission of 1974 recommended a tapering set of awards, ranging from nearly 40 percent at the bottom of the scale to 5 percent at the top – the government later reduced this latter to one of only 2 percent.[31] The setting up of these commissions clearly indicated that the state was gropping for a solution but unable to settle on anyone. This is also evident in other areas, for example, numerous commissions of investigations which were set up but whose recommendations were rarely if ever carried out.[32]

Meanwhile the miners were again awarded wage increases in 1975 and 1976 without even raising a spectre of a strike. Clearly the miners had established themselves as a powerful segment of the working class but in so doing they also helped other fractions of the working class in a 'demonstration effect' sort of way, to claim higher wages, albeit lower than those of the miners. Even while the workers were achieving higher wages, they did not regard them as fair wages, in fact according to the research done by Michael Burawoy on the mineworkers, they perceived the union leadership, white management and the black government as three pillars of the corporate 'power elite' determined to exploit and sap the workers of their energy in the pursuit of increased profits to be used as much for their own private benefit as for the development of the country.[33] Complained one semi-skilled informant:

I do not know what is happening with our Government. During the Colonial days we were getting a Copper bonus and now this has been abolished and the Mining Companies say that it has absorbed the bonus into our salaries but we see no difference. Then recently we have been cheated that there has been a 5 percent increase. We tried to complain to management but it only said, 'Your Government has a 51 percent share and we only have 49 percent, therefore if you want to complain then go to the Union'. Then we went to the Union and they said, 'If you are tired of the job go home and cultivate the land'. All this is annoying us and so we intend to withdraw our membership of the union. All the unionists are Government supporters and I suspect that the mine management gives them money to cover up its evils in dealing with our genuine complaints.[34]

Further complaints by the semi-skilled were typical:

... We ought to be getting more [money] now because production is high and we work harder than previously. ... Independence and nationalization have not changed anything. In fact things are just as they were. Moreover we work harder than we used to do in the Federal days. Pay scales are very low. The Union and the Companies together with Government have brought in pay groups which have cut all the scales and cutting allowances. Things are going down and down. We should be getting more money because we are producing more copper.[35]

This clearly shows the lower ranking workers were aware of the divergence of interests between them and the Union, Management and Government. It is not surprising that miners went on strike in 1966, 1969 and threatened to go on strike in 1971 to protest Union Compromise regarding wages with Management in 1964, 1966, 1969 and 1970. This could be an example of mineworkers' perception of the existence of a labour aristocracy leading them.

What has been reviewed above clearly shows as Bates has also shown that the state failed to turn the working class from "consumptionism" to "productionism". The working class pursued wage demands relentlessly. They thought they were producing but not consuming enough. The state's attempts at an incomes, salaries and wages policy never materialized despite the setting up of many commissions.

That the workers demanded and got wage increases however does not mean they were therefore incorporated into the state's "ideology of developmentalism" or that they therefore became a "labour aristocracy" en mass. While it is true that the state co-opted a good number of trade unionists, and trade union leadership generally opposed wildcat strikes,[36] it did not necessarily mean that workers' general interests were not served by the unions or that the rank and file also toyed the state line. In our view the fact that the rank and file continued to press for higher wages and continued to strike, clearly points to the untenability of the perspective which holds that labour was incorporated. Further if there was any incorporation of the labour aristocracy as per Parpart and Shaw, this simply did not affect wage demands and strikes by lower ranking workers. It is not surprising that to assert its interests, the state had to resort to repressive measures e.g. detention of union leaders starting in 1970. Working class struggles had to be tightly and forcibly controlled since the strategy of incorporation had clearly failed.

To help achieve this desire the state enacted the *Industrial Relations Act* in 1971. This is the subject of the next chapter. But before we move on to the next chapter, we need to point out a few things regarding the state's other activities which had justified its attempts to control the working class. The major issue as already seen was the question of rapid economic development – principally in the rural sector.

Rural Development

Since the bureaucratic bourgeoisie were very concerned about the urban and rural disparities, it is only reasonable if they were genuine in their concern, to radically alter the relations in the countryside by promoting rural development, raising wages, giving incentives to rural households etc. How then did the government perform in the rural sector?

Since Independence in 1964, the state in Zambia has attempted various programmes to improve the standard of living of the majority of the rural people. But without much success. As the 1975 I.L.O. study concludes:

> In contrast with the Government's declaration about the urgency of the need to transform the rural sector, and the priority to be given to rural development in national planning, one is struck by a neglect of agriculture, by the low priority given to rural activities in the allocation of economic resources and skilled manpower, and, overall, by the absence of clear and coherent framework for rural development, within which decisions are taken.[37]

One of the problems certainly was the absence of a clear and coherent framework for development. Notice for example the succession of strategies most of which were abandoned in mid-air in favour of new ones which also met the same fate. In 1965 the state initiated the cooperative movement and pumped a lot of money into it. The movement grew to a peak of 1,121 cooperatives in 1969 from which it started dwindling to 700 in 1979. It has been observed that cooperatives have mainly benefited the local economic and political notables rather than the poor peasants and as such have been deemed a failure in terms of raising rural incomes.[38]

Settlement Schemes, Rural Reconstruction Centres, Intensive Development Zones, the Multi-purpose Cooperatives and the Lima Programme have all failed to create rural employment opportunities and to increase quantity and coverage of peasants' incomes. In fact what happened was the reverse:

1.   The creation of parastatal organizations to oversee rural development led to the growth and expansion of the parastatal-based bourgeoisie. The Parastatals, Rural Development Corporation (RDC); National Agricultural Marketing Board (NAMBOARD), Tobacco Board of Zambia (TBZ), Cold Storage Board of Zambia (CSBZ), Dairy Produce Board of Zambia (DPBZ), and Credit Organization of Zambia (COZ) replaced by the Agricultural Finance Company (AFC) after 1969 acted more as transmission belts of state funds for private embourgeoisement of the top employees. The Mwanakatwe Salaries Commission (1975) discovered that the public service blossomed from 21,863 in 1963 to 58,013 in 1974. Superscale positions, i.e. the group from which the bureaucratic bourgeoisie spring, rose from 184 in 1962 to 1,298 in 1975 and personnel emoluments rose from K33,

563, 424 in 1964/5 to K109,952,959 in 1975.[39] The Parastatal growth in these areas was also spectacular. These parastatals also siphoned off resources from rural peasants for the benefit of the urban consumer and ultimately for the bourgeoisie. The producer prices for the agricultural products were deliberately kept low only to be sold to the urban consumer at a subsidized price. In return the peasant producer had to buy agricultural inputs e.g. implements, fertilizers etc. at a higher price. So much for the concern of the rural dweller by the state bourgeoisie. It does not show in actual practice.

2. State loans and provision of incentives to the countryside contributed to the growth and expansion of an agricultural bourgeoisie i.e. the already well privileged commercial farmers mostly along the line of rail rather than improving the lot of the people.

By the seventies, Government lack of serious inclination to uplift the countryside had already shown. The First National Development Plan (FNDP-1966-1970) was urban-oriented. While it sought to diversify the economy by reducing its dependence on copper, it did so by focusing on construction, services and manufacturing rather than on agriculture. Infrastructure and transport were allocated 38% of the total investment, industry and mining 21% and social services 18%, while agriculture received only about 12%. The Second National Development Plan (SNDP-1972-1976) allocated agriculture only 11% of total investment.[40] Capital investments in agriculture-based parastatals were declining in successive years, from K33,754,000 in 1972; K17,616,000 in 1973; K10,887,000 in 1974 and lesser amounts in the following years.[41] This lessening interest in agriculture can also be seen by looking at the share of agricultural expenditures as a percentage of total government expenditures, as Table 5.5 shows:

Table 5.5

Share of agricultural expenditures (excluding agricultural subsidies) in total Government expenditures, 1970-80

1970	1971	1972	1973	1974	1975	1976	1977	1978	1979	1980
6.2%	6.4%	5.1%	4.4%	4.6%	3.5%	3.5%	4.4%	5.3%	5.3%	4.8%

Source: ILO, *Zambia; Basic Needs in an Economy Under Pressure*, p. 219.

Compared to other subsaharan Countries, this expenditure in agriculture was one of the lowest.[42] Agriculture's contribution to GDP needlessly to say also declined, from 13.7% in 1965 to 9.4% in 1974. With two-thirds of the agricultural share originating in the traditional peasant sector, this means Zambia's two-thirds population working in traditional rural occupations earned only 6% of Zambia's National Income. In the same period, agriculture's contribution to exports declined from 2.3% in 1964 to 1.4% in 1974, while the value of food imports increased from K18 million to K45 million.[43]

In conclusion to this section, we simply point out that the typical rural dweller is much poorer now than at any time since Independence. By 1973 the minimum wage for farm labourers was about half that of unskilled workers in industry. The ratio between the lowest wage of workers in industry and the highest salaries of managers and administrators was 1:18-20 while within the civil service the ratio was 1:25. Thus the state had not succeeded in either narrowing the gaps between rural and urban incomes or within the urban areas. In the meantime just 2 percent of all Zambian families accounted for 20 percent of national household income, roughly the same share as that of the poorest 50%. Zambia had indeed become what the Ottaways have referred to as an "upper class welfare state".[44] The ILO study concluded that between 1964 and 1973 the purchasing power of the typical unit of peasant produce had fallen by 20%. In other words, a peasant farmer who responded to state calls for higher productivity, and increased his volume of sales of produce by 20%, was no better off in 1973 than he was in 1964.[45] In other words, he was worse off. The government despite the rhetoric to the contrary had shown very little inclination to salvage the situation. It has not done much to reduce the rural-urban disparities. As a matter of fact the peasants just like workers have been used as producers of wealth for the urban-based bourgeoisie, local and international. The ILO study also concluded that there was "an urgent need in Zambia to narrow the gaps; gaps between policies and their implementation, between words and action, between rich and poor, between rural and urban areas, and between the [bureaucratic bourgeoisie] and the mass of the people – mainly rural".[46]

Worker Assessment of the Sixties

Most labour leaders answering the questionnaire I had sent them indicated that the 1960s were the most agreeable in terms of the relationship between the State and the labour movement. The reasons as to why it was so differ from leader to leader. Ignatius M. Kasumbu of the National Union of Commercial and Industrial Workers (NUCIW) said that "[Between] 1964 and 1969, the relationship [between the Government and the Labour Movement] was good [because] some top leadership [of the labour movement] was considered for party government posts".[47] Timothy Walamba of the Mineworkers Union of Zambia (MUZ) says that the most agreeable period between the party govern-ment and the labour movement including MUZ was during the struggle for independence and up to 1966. From there the relationship was downhill, according to Walamba. The reason for the change tends to confirm the views of those who have regarded the MUZ as constituting a labour aristocracy as well as a right wing opposition with a reactionary foreign policy towards Southern Africa.[48] According to Walamba: "the Government decision to close the South African trade links brought about disastrous effects on the workers. Goods which used to come from the South stopped to come. Locally produced goods became expensive because of monopoly. Machinery on the mines became obsolete due to lack of spare parts. Foreign policy decisions and choice of national ideology proved to be total disasters as copper prices started to fall".[49] These policies affected workers' interests negatively and in turn caused the relationship between the Government and the labour movement to sour. Fair objective assessment.

According to M. K. Sumani of the Mineworkers Union of Zambia (MUZ), the relationship between the Government and the labour movement was agreeable between 1964 and 1973 because the Government recognized the importance of a well organized labour movement.[50] Without a well organized and recognizable labour movement, there would be industrial chaos as there would be no visible leaders the Government would negotiate with in times of industrial conflict. There were some issues that caused a lot of disagreement between the labour movement and the Government, according to Muvoywa M. Kaiko of the Zambia National Union of Teachers (ZNUT). Such were the cases as the 1968 and 1969 Copperbelt teachers' strikes and the 1970 national teachers' strike which saw the invocation of emergency powers to detain ZNUT leaders. Kaiko says that, "in each case, the Ministry of Education was held responsible for causing strikes". Another cause of disagreement according to Kaiko was the introduction of the one-party state in Zambia in the early seventies.[51] "On certain occasions the labour movement has been suspected of being infiltrated by outside influences trying to destabilise the nation"[52] which has caused some strains between the Government and the labour movement. In reality however, the Government has not been able to show outside influences in the labour movement. This was all part of an ideological offensive as an instrument of class struggle by the bureaucratic bourgeoisie.

In the next chapter, we discuss how the State dealt with the working class in the seventies and eighties in the context of the one-party state system. My assessment is that in the sixties and early seventies, the State clearly failed to suppress working class struggles and that may be why some labour leaders found the period from independence to 1970 as agreeable. The labour movement held the edge in terms of wages. By 1970, the State was becoming repressive.

Notes

1.   Kenneth Good, "The Reproduction of weakness in the state and agriculture: The Zambian experience" *African Affairs* Vol.85, No.339, 1986, p. 254. See also Morris Szeffel, "Political Graft and the Spoils System in Zambia – the State as a Resource in Itself" *Review of African Political Economy* No.24, 1982.

2.   *Times of Zambia*, 29 March, 1983.

3.   Kenneth Kaunda, *Zambia's Economic Revolution*, Address by His Excellency The President Dr. K. D. Kaunda at Mulungushi, 19th April, 1968, known as Mulungushi Declaration, (Lusaka: Government Printer, 1969).

4.   Kenneth Kaunda, *Zambia Towards Economic Independence* Speech given at the National Council of the United National Independence Party at Matero on 11th August, 1969, known as the Matero Declaration, (Lusaka: Government Printer, 1969). 5.Marcia Burdette, *The Dynamics of Nationalization Between Multinational Companies and Peripheral States: Negotiations Between Amax Inc., The Anglo American Corporation of South Africa, Ltd., and the Government of Zambia* Ph.D. Dissertation, Columbia University, 1979.

6.   Zambia Daily Mail, 17 September, 1982.

7.   See Greg Lanning and Marti Mueller, *Africa Undermined: Mining Companies and the Underdevelopment of Africa*, (Harmondsworth: Penguin, 1979) pp. 196-229.

8.   Burdette, note 5 and Lanning and Mueller, note 7.

9.   "The Beginning of Class Consciousness" *Times of Zambia*, 9 September, 1969. See also "President Condemns Class Cleavages" in *Zambia's Guideline for the Next Decade* H. E., the President, Dr. Kenneth Kaunda Addressing the National Council of UNIP, Mulungushi, 9 November, 1968, p. 17, Zambia Information Services, Lusaka, 1968.

10.   "President warns of Dangers of a Labour Aristocracy" *Towards Complete Independence*, Speech by H.E., The President D. K. Kaunda to the UNIP National Council held at Matero Hall, Lusaka, 11 August, 1969, Zambia Information Services, Lusaka, pp. 44-45.

11.   Ibid.

12.   Ibid.

13.   Cherry Gertzel, "Labour and State: The Case of Zambia's Mineworkers Union" *Journal of Commonwealth and Comparative Politics* 13, 3, 1975, p. 290.

14.   Gertzel Ibid.

15.   See Ackson Kanduza, "Teachers' strike 1970: A Chapter in Zambia's Labour History" in *The Evolving Structure of Zambian Society*, University of Edinburgh, Centre of African Studies, 1980, pp. 281-295 and Robin Fincham

and Grace Zulu "Labour and Participation in Zambia" in *Development in Zambia*, edited by Ben Turok, (London: Zed., 1981) pp. 214-227.

16. Issa G. Shivji "Preface" in *The State and the Working People in Tanzania* edited by Issa G. Shivji, (Dakar: Codesria, 1985). Further, for a good study of this theme, see Issa G. Shivji, *Law, State and the Working Class in Tanzania*, (London: James Currey, 1986).

17. *Report of the Commission Appointed to Review the Salaries and Conditions of Service of the Northern Rhodesia Public and Teaching Services, and of the Northern Rhodesia Army and Air Force* (Hadow Commission Report) (Lusaka: Government Printer, 1964).

18. Report of the Commission of Inquiry into the Mining Industry (Brown Commission Report) Lusaka, 1966, Quoted in James Fry, *Employment and Income Distribution in the African Economy*, (London: Groom Helm Ltd., 1979) p. 107.

19. Whelan Civil Service Salaries Commission (Lusaka: Government Printer, 1966).

20. Fry, note 18, p. 109.

21. Report to the Government of Zambian Incomes, Wages, and Prices Policy and Machinery (Firt Turner Report), (Lusaka: Government Printer, 1969).

22. Fry, note 18, p. 110.

23. *Zambia News*, 31 July, 1970.

24. C. A. Rogers (Chairman), *Administrative Working Party Appointed to Examine Certain Aspects of the Teaching Service*, Education in Transition, Lusaka, 1969; H. J. Soko (Chairman) *Report of the Board of Inquiry to look into the causes and Circumstances Leading to the Existence of a Trade Dispute Between the Zambia National Union of Teachers and the Ministry of Education*, Lusaka: 1970 and Kanduza, note 15.

25. Kanduza, note 15.

26. Cherry Gertzel, "Labour and the State" in *Some Aspects of Zambian Labour Relations*, (Lusaka: National Archives of Zambia, 1975) p. 142.

27. See Kanduza, note 15.

28. *Zambia Daily Mail*, 14th October, 1971.

29. Fry, note 18, p. 111.

30. Report of the Commission Appointed to Review the Salaries, Salary Structure and Conditions of Service of the Zambia Public Service (O'Riordan Commission Report), (Lusaka: Government Printer, 1971).

31. *Report of the Commission of Inquiry into Salaries, Salary Structure and Conditions of Service, Vol. One, The Public Services and the Parastatal Sector* (Mwanakatwe Commission Report), (Lusaka: Government Printer, 1975).

32. Klaas Woldring "Corruption and Inefficiency - Problems Galore! Survey of Recent Inquiries and Their Results" in *Beyond Political Indepen-*

dence: Zambia's Development Predicament in the 1980s, ed. by Klaas Woldring and Chibwe Chibaye, (Berlin et al.: Mouton, 1984) pp. 183-209.

33. Michael Burawoy, "Another Look at the Mineworker" *African Social Research* 14, 1972 p.263.

34. Ibid., p. 262.

35. Ibid., pp. 262-263.

36. "Dangers of Wildcat Strikes" *Times of Zambia*, 29th January, 1971.

37. International Labour Office, *Norrowing The Gaps: Planning for Basic Needs and Productive Employment in Zambia*, (Addis Ababa: JASPA, 1977), Quoted in Klaas Woldring, "The Rural Malaise in Zambia: Reflection on the Rene Dumont Report and the State Farms Project" in *Beyond Political Independence*, note 32, p. 99.

38. Ibid.

39. M. C. Bwalya, "Participation or Powerlessness: The Place of Peasants in Zambia's Rural Development" in *Beyond Political Independence*, note 32, p. 79.

40. David and Marina Ottaway, *Afrocommunism*, (New York: Africana Publishing Company, 1981) p. 40.

41. Bwalya, note 39, p. 76.

42. See Munyonzwe Hamalengwa, "L'accumulation Primitive Et la Reproduction De La Population Rural En Afrique" in *Le Village Et Le Bidonville: Retention Et Migration des Populations Rurales d'Afrique* ed. Jose Havet, (Ottawa: Editions de L'Universite d'Ottawa, 1986) pp. 76-101.

43. Narrowing the Gaps, note 37, p. 76.

44. Ottaway, note 40, pp. 37-44.

45. Quoted in Ottaway, note 40, p. 39.

46. Ibid.

47. Ignatius M. Kasumbu, NUCIW (March 16, 1987).

48. Discussion with Joseph Hanlon, Freelance Journalist, Toronto, March 1987.

49. Timothy Walamba, MUZ (March 11, 1987).

50. M. K. Sumani, MUZ (March 11, 1987). See also on this point M.B.N. Nguvu, "The Role of Trade Unions and Employers' Organizations in Socio-Economic Development and Employment Promotion in Zambia", (Geneva, International Institute for Labour Studies, 1 EME 3112, 1976).

51. Muvoywa M. Kaiko, ZNUT (March 16, 1987).

52. Ibid.

6

Class Struggles in Zambia, Phase 2, 1971 – 1976:
The Industrial Relations Act

I call the period from 1971 to 1976 phase 2, because that is when the State brought in the most comprehensive and all encompassing piece of labour legislation to date – the *Industrial Relations Act* (IRA), 1971. This Act can be regarded as an attempt by the State to seal the loopholes that had shown themselves vis-a-vis working class struggles in the first period. In this chapter I first deal with the relevant sections of the Act and then move on to assessing to what extent the Act has been successful in bringing about the desired results.

The IRA repealed the *Trade Unions and Trade Disputes Ordinances* and the *Industrial Conciliation Ordinance* which had governed labour relations hitherto. They were deemed inadequate to deal with complex labour relations and hence needed to be replaced.

The Zambian Industrial Relations Act, 1971 was deemed the most advanced piece of labour legislation in English-speaking Africa.[1] The Act was brought into force by Statutory Instrument No.29 of 1974, with the exception of Part VII concerning Works Councils (WCs). This latter part came into operation in 1976 after massive resistance from management of various work places.

The idea of a comprehensive Industrial Relations Act was introduced by President Kaunda at the 1969 Second National Convention of the ruling party, United National Independence Party (UNIP) at Kitwe, ostensibly "to change the whole system of industrial relations [in Zambia] so that our workers can effectively participate in the decisions of management ... it was time to establish relations between the worker and the employer that [were] in keeping with the philosophy of Humanism".[2] The period from 1969 to 1971 was a period of consultation, preparation and education of the working class on the proposed Industrial Relations Act. Thus the proposed Act was sold to workers as the main beneficiaries in the form of their participation in the proposed Works Councils (WCs) which would provide the machinery within the undertaking for their participation in management decisions. But caveats were included which showed the real intentions of the proposed Act, "To a large extent the new system of industrial relations will put the onus on the workers to discipline themselves. If they refuse to accept this responsibility, they will destroy our economy and themselves with it". The Act promised more, as the President went on to say, "The new law will for the first time abolish the hated system of master and servant. For the first time workers and managers will be equal partners in industry". There was also a warning, "this means that the coming of age of the workers will at last be legally recognized. From adults one expects adult behaviour".[3]

The Industrial Relations Act (No.36 of 1971)[4]

"An Act to provide for the registration of trade unions; the Zambia Congress of Trade Unions, the Employers' Associations and the Zambia Federation of employers; to provide for the establishment of Works Councils, collective agreements, the settlement of collective disputes and the establishment of an Industrial Relations Court; to repeal certain enactments relating to trade unions and trade disputes and industrial conciliation; and to provide for matters incidental to or connected with the foregoing".

The IRA is divided into eleven parts containing one hundred and twenty-five sections altogether; Part One (Sections 1-4) is a preliminary introductory statement dealing with title of the Act, to whom it appeals; interpretation; Part Two (Sections 5-25) deals with the registration of trade unions; Part Three (Sections 26-28) deals with the Zambia Congress of Trade Unions; Part Four (Section 29) pertains to control of funds of trade unions, congress (ZCTU), employers' associations and the Federation of Employers. Part Five (Sections 30-51) deals with Employers' Associations while Part Six (Sections 52-53) pertains to the Zambia Federation of Employers (ZFE). Part Seven (Sections 54-78) deals with works councils; Part Eight (Sections 79-88) relates to Joint Councils and collective agreements; Part Nine (Sections 89-95) pertains to the settlement of collective disputes. Part Ten (Sections 96-109) deals with the Industrial Relations Court and lastly Part Eleven (Sections 116-125) pertains to general residual questions.

Using the language of the Act, it can be stated that the objectives of the Act, even if they are not neatly defined are:[5]

1. To minimise the causes of industrial unrest by encouraging and protecting freedom of association for both employees and employers. Section 4 protects the right of employees to take part in the formation of a trade union and be members of such a trade union, if they so desire. Section 31 protects the right of employers to participate in the formation of, and to join, or not to join, an association, to participate in the lawful activities of such an association and to become members of any such lawful association.

2. To promote sound and stable industrial peace by the settlement of issues respecting terms and conditions of employment through collective bargaining. Section 82 imposes on bargaining units the duty to negotiate with the management of the undertaking for the purpose of concluding a new collective agreement before the expiration of an existing collective agreement.

3. To encourage and promote the settlement of disputes in an orderly and efficient manner by prescribing the procedure and the machinery for settling them. In Part IX, Section 89 sets down the situation under which a collective dispute is deemed to exist; Section 91 provides for mediation; Section 93 for conciliation and Section 95 for final settlement by the Industrial Relations Court, if other methods have failed.

4. To discourage and prevent unfair labour practices such as infringing on the freedom of association; dismissing or discriminating against any employee for filing charges or giving testimony under the Industrial Relations Act (Section 4-2); a company assisting a trade union with money (Section 4-3); and discrimination in employment (Section 114).

5. To promote effective workers' participation and to secure mutual co-operation, "in the interests of industrial peace, improved working conditions, greater efficiency and productivity" – given in Section 69 as the objectives of Works Councils.

In short the Act was intended to promote industrial pluralism in Zambia. If we abandon the legalistic language of the Act it immediately becomes clear that the Act was intended to control and domesticate the working class by among others, erecting lengthy bureaucratic procedures for the settlement of disputes; by severely restricting the right to strike; by imposing a long list of "essential services" in which strikes were illegal; by restricting the powers of trade unions, for example some of their work being taken over by Works Councils ostensibly for the promotion of industrial peace but in reality to weaken trade unions; by requiring the final settlement to be decided by the Industrial Relations Court whose decisions were final, binding and could not be appealed; the provision for complete intervention by the State in industrial relations, etc. There were however many positive aspects to the Act which could benefit workers as it will be made clear below. The point, however, that I want to stress is that if the Act was implemented the way it was designed, if all the procedures and processes for collective bargaining were followed and if the working class obeyed all the stipulations about not going on strike in "essential services", etc. then the Act would have the effect of domesticating the working class. The Act as a whole could be regarded as an instrument of class struggle by the bureaucratic bourgeoisie against the working class. Let me elaborate by looking at specific areas of the Act which I believe would have the effect of domesticating the working class if its provisions were to be strictly adhered to. I will later include the assessments of the Act by the leaders of the labour movement itself.

The Zambia Congress of Trade Unions

Every registered trade union in Zambia was required by the Act to affiliate to the ZCTU. Before this Act, there was no compulsory affiliation. All affiliated unions were also now required to pay 30% of their accrued monies to the ZCTU. Further since ZCTU was affiliated to the ruling party – United National Independence Party (UNIP) in 1971, this meant that indirectly if not directly union members and rank and file also now belonged to UNIP. Since all members of UNIP were required to obey party rules and to owe allegiance to the party president, who was also president of the country, adherence to trade union matters could become blurred in favour of party matters. This even became more so with the coming into existence of the one-party state in 1973. The one-party state imposed that if any one wanted to stand for elections, he needed to be a member of UNIP. This obviously had the effect of limiting freedom of association, freedom of free political activity etc. We shall see later how this affected 17 prominent trade unionists who were expelled from UNIP in 1981. One of these was a member of parliament and because of his expulsion from UNIP on an unrelated matter to his parliamentary conduct, he also lost his seat in parliament. It was also feared for sometime that these trade unionists had lost their trade union posts.

ZCTU was given further powers in 1973 by the Minister of Labour and Social Services. By *Statutory Instrument 216 of 1973* the Minister expanded ZCTU powers among others to include the right to take part in any negotiations between employers and an affiliated trade union. Secondly, before any negotiations at industry level involving wages and other conditions of employment, the trade union concerned was required to submit its proposals to the Executive Committee of Congress who had the right to vary such proposals and give specific and general directions to the member trade union on matters of policy. Thirdly whenever ZCTU decided on a matter submitted to it by an affiliated trade union, its decision was binding on ZCTU and the member trade union, provided that decision was not contrary to any written law.

The danger with these powers given to ZCTU was that if the ZCTU leadership was incorporated into the State's ideology, it would by these powers neutralize working class demands. These powers were one indication of the State's attempts to incorporate the working class through ZCTU. The problematic however was, what happened to these powers if ZCTU was not totally incorporated? We will examine this issue below when we deal with the actual effects or lack of effects of the State's attempts at incorporating the working class through the Industrial Relations Act (IRA).

Trade Unions

The *Industrial Relations Act*, Section 3(2) defines a trade union as:

> a combination of employees which is registered as a trade union under *Section five* and includes the local branch executive of a trade union, representing employees in an undertaking, and under the *constitution* of which principal objects are the regulation of collective relations between employees and employers, or between employers and organisations of employers or between employees and employees, which said objects are – referred to as statutory objects.

Section 5(3) stipulated that every trade union was required to register with the Labour Commissioner within six months from the date of its formation. If the Labour Commissioner refused to register a trade union, it had to dissolve within six months from "the date of its formation or the date of notification by the Commissioner to the trade union of such refusal", otherwise every officer was liable to a fine of up to K10.00 for every day the union continued illegally and/or to imprisonment for up to 6 months.

The Industrial Relations Act required that all trade union constitutions should be registered with the Labour Commissioner who at the same time was the Registrar of Trade Unions. Every trade union constitution must have among its rules the following statutory matters:

1. the name of the trade union and its registered office in Zambia,

2. the principal objects of that trade union and the class of employee it is to represent,

3. the purpose to which union funds shall be used which *must* include workers' education purposes,

4. the organisational structure of that trade union and the method of appointing and removal of office bearers, also their powers,

5. the amount of entrance fees and subscriptions and method of collecting such funds from members, and grounds for disqualifying a member from voting on any trade union matter,

6. the vesting and safe custody of union funds and property, banking, auditing of its accounts and financial records,

7. disqualification for election of officers of the trade union and the appointments as well as their removal from office,

8. the election of officers of trade union after six months of its formation and thereafter at intervals not exceeding four years,

9. the appointment of trade union trustees of not less than two and not more than four,

10. the taking of decisions on union matters by secret ballot supervised in every case by an independent person appointed by the trade union.

In Zambia, Trade Unions are industrial, that is they organize all workers in a single industry or factory or work-place regardless of the type of work that they do or the amount of skill they have. During the Colonial era, Trade Unions were initially based on skills a worker possessed. The unskilled were excluded from membership. Industrial unions have one great advantage according to J. S. Mazyopa of ZCTU: "their economic strength. When economic strength must be used, all the workers in the workplace respond. This gives great strength".[6]

The organisational structure of Trade Unions in Zambia including ZCTU is generally the same in terms of categories of office bearers, National, Regional, District, Branch and Factory levels as the case may be. There is a General Council where the full-time administrators of the trade unions are elected. Generally this is composed of: The National Chairman, Deputy National Chairman, General Secretary, Deputy General Secretary, Treasurer, Deputy Treasurer and Trustees. The General Council is attended by delegates from the Regional, District and Branch levels as the case may be. The organizational structure in this regard is as follows:

General Council
|
Executive Council
|
Secretariat
|
Regional Level
|
District Level
|
Branch Level
|
Factory Level

This set up can have far-reaching repercussions in terms of government policies on labour. What pertains to state attempts at incorporating trade unions has already been implied above i.e. since trade unions were required by law to be affiliated to ZCTU and if ZCTU was incorporated into the ideology of the State and used its powers given by the Minister of Labour and Social Services by Statutory instrument 216 of 1973, affiliated trade unions would likely be weakened, especially the already weaker and smaller unions. This would set the stage for State incorporation of trade unions. This however has not been the case. ZCTU does not control the unions and it and the Zambian State are dissatisfied about this. ZCTU has stated that strength in real terms belongs to the unions and not to ZCTU; affiliated unions are autonomous organizations with their own rules; the ZCTU has no authority over individual members of its affiliates except through the authority of those affiliates; and the congress cannot instruct unions nor can it control strikes without the co-operation of the unions concerned.[7] Unions do not always manage to control the rank and file members. Despite this, however the dangers remain that unions could be incorporated through ZCTU, if and when ZCTU was weakened.

One other method the State used to attempt to incorporate the trade union leadership was through manipulation of union elections so that a pliable leadership could be elected. This has been the case as already alluded to, especially with regards to elections in MUZ, the most powerful union in the country. However, even if a pliable leadership was in control, the rank and file has often subverted the leadership by going on wild-cat strikes.

Collective Bargaining, Dispute Settlement and Collective Agreement

"Freedom of Association" was guaranteed in Section 4 to employees in terms of having the right: to help form a trade union; to join a trade union; to be active in a trade union; and, to hold office in a trade union. Procedures for collective bargaining and for handling collective disputes were established in parts VIII and IX of the Act. However, there were severe government constraints on the freedom of action of trade unions. Section 117 forbade strikes and lock-outs in the long list of essential services which were set up in Section 3:

1. any service relating to the generation, supply or distribution of electricity;

2. any fire brigade or fire service;

3. any sewerage, rubbish disposal or other sanitation service;

4. any health, hospital or ambulance service;

5. any service relating to the supply or distribution of water;

6. any service relating to the production, supply, delivery or distribution of food or fuel;

7. mining, including any service required for the working of a mine;

8. any communications service;

9. any transport service, and any service relating to the repair and maintenance or to the driving, loading and unloading, of vehicle for use in the transport service;

10. any road, railway, bridge, ferry, pontoon, airfield, harbour or dock;

11. any other service or facility, whether or not of a kind similar to the foregoing, declared by the President to be a necessary service for the purposes of and under the Preservation of Public Security Regulations or any other Regulations or enactment replacing the same.

The list can be extended by Presidential decree under the Preservation of Public Security Regulations.

It is difficult to envisage any work situation that would not be covered directly or indirectly by this list. The President could add more work places on the list if he so desired. Any strike or lock-out in any of these places was illegal. Any contravention carried heavy penalties, either fines or a prison term. If this list was strictly adhered to by the workers, there would be no strikes in Zambia. Note that the list includes Mining and Transport (especially railways) two of the industries with the most active labour unions in the country. Timothy Walamba of MUZ has complained that the Act "unfortunately lists down all workers in the country as essential workers who cannot be allowed to go on strike".[8] This would muzzle workers' most potent weapon – strike. Where the right to strike in other industries is implied (e.g. Section 8j ii), Section 115 and Section 116(2a) it is very severely restricted by the other provisions of Section 116(2):

No employee, trade union or other person shall take part in a strike which:

1. has not been authorized by a strike ballot taken in the manner provided by the constitution of a trade union;

2. is not in contemplation or furtherance of a collective dispute, to which such employee or trade union is a party; or

3. is in contemplation or furtherance of a collective dispute in which conciliation is in progress or which has been referred to the Industrial Relations Court for its decision. Section 116(2a) above rules out wild-cat strikes. Section 116(2c) is in contemplation of a long bureaucratic process a collective dispute goes through before a strike can be called, which effectively rules out strikes. Walamba has remarked that "the Act gives workers the right to strike after following established channels (which in any case are impossible to follow)",[9] meaning there is no substantive legal right to strike in Zambia. It is not necessary to describe the long bureaucratic process a labour dispute was required to pass through which in our view tended to rule out strikes, legal or illegal.

It is only necessary to mention the role of the Industrial Relations Court. If conciliation fails, the Conciliator (or Chairman of the Board of Conciliators) reports in writing the issues of disagreement to the Minister, who refers the entire dispute to the Industrial Relations Court.[10] The Court then makes its decision which shall be final and binding.[11] It has already been pointed out that Section 116 prohibits lockouts and strikes "in contemplation or furtherance of a collective dispute in which conciliation is in progress or which has been referred to the Industrial Relations Court for its decision". Section 116 read in conjunction with Part IX would also appear to rule out lock-outs and strikes as instruments of collective bargaining, except possibly before the conciliation stage and just possibly, under Section 94-5, where the Court decides that the written settlement, in whole or in part, is contrary to law. In which case, the parties are expected to renegotiate the provision declared unlawful by the Court. The process would start all over again and at the end, the Court's decision is final and binding. Therefore the provisions of the IRA rule out strikes, perhaps the most important instrument of class struggle short of revolutionary action possessed by the working class. We shall see below how effective or not the State has been in preventing working class actions.

The Industrial Relations Court

The addition of the IRC in the IRA is the most notable innovation in Zambian industrial relations scene. The Court has powers to: *(a)* examine and approve collective agreements.[12] *(b)* give awards and decisions in collective disputes and with respect to industrial relations matters referred to the Court.[13] *(c)* interpret awards and agreements[14] and resolve all ambiguities.[15] *(d)* deal with appeals,[16] *(e)* declare who is/should be the holder of an office in a trade union; ZCTU; Employers' Association or Zambia Federation of Employees (ZFE)[17] and issue injunctions against affected members or officers of those bodies;[18] *(f)* perform such acts and duties prescribed in this Act or any other written law;[19] *(g)* adjudicate on any matter concerning rights, duties and privileges of employees, employers, and their representative bodies; *(h)* commit to prison and punish for contempt any person disobeying or ignoring an order of the Court;[20] and *(i)* the Court's decisions and awards are final and binding upon all affected parties.[21]

If the decisions of the Court are final and binding, what other power have the workers got left? And especially since the Court (as the IRC does) has to take into account the state defined "public interest" and "policies" in its decisions! As already pointed out, the Court consults closely with the State personnel i.e. the Minister of Labour and Social Services and the Labour Commissioner, in addition to the officers of the Court being appointed by the President thus further reducing the possibility of the impartiality of the Court. It is thus not difficult to contemplate that the IRC was deliberately set up as another barrier to working class action in the form of strikes. The lengthy conciliation process followed by the final and binding decision of the Court reached after consultation with the State (Minister of Labour and Social Services) in the context of a one-party state political environment left no room for any other conclusion. The labour movement has criticized the role of the IRC wishing that it should only register decisions and not decide on its own. Further the labour movement wished IRC decisions could be appealed to another body, for example an Industrial Tribunal. They do not like the set up that the IRC has the final say.[22]

Works Councils

The centre piece of the IRA as it was being sold to the workers was the establishment of Works Councils through which workers were to participate in management decisions. The Works Councils are provided for in Part VII, Sections 54 to 78. To perhaps emphasize the importance attached to the Works Councils by the State, the Head of the State and Party, President Kaunda was to oversee their establishment and operation. The rest of the Act was under the Minister of Labour and Social Services. The rest of the Act came into operation as already stated on 1st April, 1974 whereas Part VII (Works Councils) was delayed until 1st May, 1976 when the President announced by *Statutory Instrument 76 of 1976* that it would become effective from that date. Thus already we can begin to feel uneasy that the very stated *raison d'etre* for the Act i.e. workers' participation was delayed for two years after the rest of the Act came into operation and with some revisions at that. We shall come to that below.

Works Councils were to comprise between 3 and 15 members with two-thirds being elected by the eligible employees and one third appointed by management.[23] The objectives of the Works Councils are: *(a)* to promote and maintain the effective participation of workers in the affairs of the undertaking, and *(b)* to secure the mutual co-operation of workers, management and trade unions in the undertaking in the interest of industrial peace, improved working conditions, greater efficiency and productivity.[24]

There were four types of "participation" by Works Councils in the running of their undertaking: *(a)* having information, in writing, of decisions by management (directors etc.) on a range of matters of policy, previously usually not openly discussed;[25] *(b) being consulted upon and participating fully and effectively in all matters of health and welfare of the eligible employees;*[26] *(c)* having "veto powers" (that is, Works Councils approval was necessary) on matters of policy in the field of personnel management and industrial relations. These powers were qualified (moderated) in various ways[27] *(d)* acting as a watch-dog regarding management contraventions of laws, rules and agreements which affected the employees of the undertaking.[28]

However, much as the Works Councils were billed as vehicles for workers' participation, there were many restrictions and limitations to what impact they could have. Some trade unionists have viewed Works Councils as threats to the work of trade unions. Section 74 is seen as giving to Works Councils duties which traditionally and statutorily belong to the trade unions.

Workers have said that "in order to avoid conflicts between Trade Unions and Works Councils, powers of Works Councils should be clearly defined".[29] For one the employee-members of the Works Councils should know the needs of the workers they represent regarding health and welfare, employee services and fringe benefits. As well as knowing these needs, they should be able to express them clearly. Further those employee members of the Works Councils should have at least a working knowledge of investments, financial control, distribution of profits, economic planning, job evaluation and wages theories in order that they may be able to understand, use and explain to the workers the information which, under the Act, management must make available to them. They should also have enough understanding of personnel management and industrial relations to be able to evaluate fairly and reasonably the management policy decisions in these fields, submitted to the Works Councils for approval. These are some of the areas trade unions have traditionally handled. Further there is no provision for working class job action as the Industrial Relations Court always steps in to give decisions which are final and binding. It would be useful to do a systematic study of the decisions of the IRC to see where the pendulum swings.[30]

Workers' Perception of the Industrial Relations Act

I alluded above to the real purposes of the IRA – as an instrument of class struggle by the state bourgeoisie against the working class. The workers however have given a more sophisticated analysis of the Act than mere class instrumentalism. Apart from some misgivings about the lengthy procedures for reaching collective agreements without strikes; the declaration of work places as "essentials"; the fact that the Industrial Relations Court has to make the final decision without appeal from it, and the conflicting roles of Works Councils and Trade Unions, the labour leaders have a positive outlook on the Industrial Relations Act. S. I. Silwimba, General Secretary of the National Union of Plantation and Agricultural Workers (NUPAW) for example says that:

> Nothing could be good for the labour movement without a law empowering them to exist and organizations representing the interests of workers ... [the IRA] has improved the recognition and provided a command to both the employer and employers' Associations to legally feel bound by law to respect the interests and welfare of Union members and their Unions.[31]

N. L. Simatendele of the Zambia National Union of Teachers (ZNUT) has echoed the same sentiments about the IRA:

It has protected the Union from being victimized by those against the existence of Trade Unions ... It has forced the employer to recognize the existence of the Union. It has also forced him to consult the Union on matters affecting workers.[32]

Asked whether the Act came to serve the Government or the workers' interests, most respondents answered that it came to serve both.[33] Some said yes and no. Simatendele has stated that it serves both parties' interests because "it has in some cases brought peace between the two parties by creating dialogue".[34] The sophistication of the answers to the question of which interests the Act was enacted to serve cautions against too ready a reading of the law as a mere malleable instrument of the ruling class. Issa Shivji, I think has captured perfectly the nature of law, particularly labour law in our case when he states:[35]

In some cases law is used as a direct instrument, tool, of the ruling class and serves its immediate interests without mediations of intermediate links. This we term as the *instrumentalist* character or aspect of law ... But at times, particular pieces of legislation may also exhibit a *political* characteristic. By political characteristic we refer to that aspect of law which en-capsulates or embodies either the results of class struggle or is meant to control class struggle. Here, too, it is *ultimately* the interests of the ruling/dominating class that are served. Yet they are mediated through and do embody certain partial successes and gains by the ruled/dominated classes. Laws on trade unions and trade-disputes settlement machinery may be said to be of this type ... (emphasis in original).

Labour leaders certainly feel that the IRA embodies partial successes for them and they have continuously strived for amendments to the Act to score more successes for the labour movement. The State bourgeoisie have also moved for amendment of the Act from time to time to reflect more their interests. In this sense, law and labour law in this case is a reflection and result of ongoing class struggles.[36]

Later there were movements to remove the threat of imprisonment from the Act; to trim down the ambit of essential services; to remove the requirement of affiliation to ZCTU and so many other amendments. Most of the amendments were initiated by the state in order to weaken the labour movement and sometimes in order to be in accord with international labour law.

In the next chapter, we look at the impact of the IRA, especially the Works Councils provisions, on class struggles in Zambia.

Notes

1.   Wogu Ananaba, *The Trade Union Movement in Africa: Promise and Performance*, (London: C. Hurst and Company, 1979) p. 180.

2.   Speech of H. E. The President Dr. K. D. Kaunda at Second National Convention, Kitwe, December, 1969. Extracts reproduced in *Industrial Relations Act Handbook* prepared by: The President's Citizenship College, Kabwe, revised edition, 1976, p. 1. Most of my analysis in this chapter unless otherwise indicated is based on information from this Handbook.

3.   Ibid.

4.   Cap. 517 of *The Laws of Zambia*, reproduced in I.L.O. *Legislative Series* No.2, March - April, 1973.

5.   See *Industrial Relations Act Handbook*, note 2, p. 4.

6.   "The Zambia Congress of Trade Unions" *The Workers Voice*, Vol.2, No.7 (September, 1979) p. 3.

7.   Wogu Ananaba, note 1, p. 59.

8.   Timothy Walamba, MUZ, (March 16, 1987).

9.   Ibid.

10.   Section 95 – 1.

11.   Section 95 – 2.

12.   Section 98(a).

13.   Section 98(b), (c).

14.   Section 98(d).

15.   Section 102.

16.   Sections 28, 37, 59, 73 – 4, 74 – 3.

17.   Section 99.

18.   Sections 17, 44.

19.   Section 98(e).

20.   Section 98(f).

21.   Section 101 – 3.

22.   See "Symposium Resolves" *The Workers Voice*, Vol.3, No.2 (September, 1980) p. 7.

23.   Section 57.

24.   Section 69.

25.   Section 71.

26.   Section 70.

27.   Sections 72, 73, 75 – 2.

28.   Section 74.

29.   The Workers Voice, note 39, p. 7.

30.   The decisions of the IRC that I have examined so far are contained in 3 volumes, 1975-1978, 1979-1981 and 1981-1983, Republic of Zambia, Ministry of Labour and Social Services. Industrial Relations Court: *The Zambia Industrial Cases Reports*.

31. S. I. Silwimba, NUPAW, (March 16, 1987).

32. N. L. Simatendele, ZNUT, (March 16, 1987).

33. Interviews and Questionnaire.

34. Simatendele, note 69.

35. Issa G. Shivji, *Law, State and the Working Class in Tanzania,* (London: James Currey, 1986) p. 3.

36. For a very interesting analysis of the law along these lines, see E. P. Thompson, *Whigs and Hunters* (New York: Pantheon, 1975.)

7

Class Struggles in Zambia, Phase 3, 1976 – 1989

I call the period after the coming into operation of the IRA, phase 3 because it marks or should mark a different era in class struggles in Zambia. I expect the IRA to have modified the character or nature of class struggle after 1976. If it has not, then it will be judged as a failure. In chapter 5, I brought the analysis of class struggle to 1975 overlapping with phase 2 (the interregnum occasioned by the IRA) and concluded that the state had failed to incorporate labour into its ideology of development. I posed that, that is why the state decided upon bringing in the IRA In chapter 6, I analyzed the various provisions of the IRA and suggested that the aim of the Act was to control and contain class struggles of the working class. In this chapter I evaluate the extent to which the intentions of the Act have been met. I look at specific issues to fathom the success or failure of the IRA

Works Councils

The works councils were introduced into the IRA as vehicles for the promotion of Industrial Participatory Democracy (IPD) of the workers.[1] Have these achieved their aim? What is the implication of the term "Participation" of the workers in management decisions? There are two broad perspectives on the implication of this term as it has been ventilated in Zambia. Firstly, proponents of participation believe that workers' horizons have hitherto been limited to issues of immediate interest to them, like pay, and that they should aspire to playing a much fuller part in the running of the organizations to which they devote so much of their lives. On the other hand, critics of participation have suggested that in the particular situations in which participation has been introduced, invariably at state or management initiative, it has been used to head off a radical upsurge in workers' demands.[2] Thus the effects of the works councils vis-a-vis workers' participation must be evaluated within the above perspectives, do they broaden democratic participation or do they stifle this participation.

So far as I am aware, there is only one independent study that has attempted to evaluate the workings of works councils in various undertakings.[3] My own study was limited to few interviews, discussions and literature survey (newspapers). I mainly rely on the above mentioned study albeit that it may be a little outdated. The picture has not changed that much. Fincham and Zulu found that there were 113 works councils in existence by 1978 and that in some private firms these existed only on paper.[4] A questionnaire on the usefulness of works councils was sent to all firms that had then formed councils. The results are tabled as follows:

Table 7.1
'The system is working well considering its short period of operation'

	Management Representatives Agreeing (MRs)	Worker Representatives Agreeing (WRs)
Private	7 (54%)	18 (82%)
Parastatal	14 (78%)	39 (66%)
Total	29 (72%)	57 (70%)

Table 7.2
'Agreement is usually reached...'

	Easily		With Difficulty		Rarely	
	MRs	WRs	MRs	WRs	MRs	WRs
Private	5 (38%)	2 (9%)	7 (54%)	14 (64%)	1 (8%)	6 (27%)
Parastatal	14 (54%)	17 (31%)	9 (35%)	30 (55%)	3 (12%)	8 (15%)
Total	19 (49%)	19 (25%)	16 (41%)	44 (57%)	4 (8%)	14 (18%)

Table 7.3
'Agreed Actions are implemented ...'

	Always		Sometimes		Seldom	
	MRs	WRs	MRs	WRs	MRs	WRs
Private	13 (100%)	4 (18%)	0 (0%)	4 (18%)	0 (0%)	14 (64%)
Parastatal	15 (57%)	8 (25%)	3 (11%)	15 (47%)	9 (33%)	9 (28%)
Total	28 (70%)	12 (27%)	3 (8%)	19 (43%)	9 (22%)	23 (30%)

Table 7.4
'When I speak on any item I feel my employment is...'

	Secure		Not Secure	
	MRs	WRs	MRs	WRs
Private	12 (92%)	10 (45%)	1 (8%)	12 (55%)
Parastatal	19 (83%)	29 (58%)	4 (17%)	21 (42%)
Total	31 (86%)	39 (54%)	5 (14%)	33 (46%)

Table 7.1 shows that there were differences between respondents from the parastatal and private sectors. Management representatives from private firms were least enthusiastic about the Councils, and workers in private firms were most enthusiastic. On the other hand, in the parastatals, management representatives were a little more enthusiastic than workers. Fincham and Zulu think that the latter probably reflects the fact that councils in parastatals have generally been established by initiative from the top (i.e. by parastatal based bourgeoisie) and that workers are for the most part relatively well represented by other mechanisms, e.g. party committees and trade unions.[5] Our investigations indicate that those councils that are introduced from the top are feared by workers because they are regarded as a strategy of incorporation of workers and subversive of trade union work.[6]

Table 7.2 shows that management representatives on the whole were markedly less critical of cooperation at meetings than were workers; management representatives in private undertakings were rather more critical than those in parastatals. A similar pattern applied to workers. The finding is thus that it seems that councils in private undertakings experience the most conflict in decision-making.

Table 7.3 establishes that when it comes to the question of frequency with which agreed actions are implemented, there is a split in management and worker judgement. Whereas 70% of management felt that "agreed actions" were "always" implemented, 73% of workers felt that they were only implemented "sometimes" or "seldom". Note also that management in private enterprises were less enthusiastic about the councils in the first place, but most enthusiastic in implementing decisions (100%) agreed about by an institution whose existence they were less enthusiastic about in the first place! Is that not a massive contradiction? You would expect them to be less enthusiastic about implementing decisions made by an institution they did not like that much. Or could it be that they bulldozed them in order to readily implement them? On the other hand 18% of the workers in private firms agreed that "agreed actions were always implemented". When it comes to freedom of participation in the councils and the implication thereof, Table 7.4 establishes that 46% of worker representatives felt insecure about their employment and more insecurity was expressed in private firms.

The conclusion is that councillors thought of councils as useful though not consensual bodies. Manager councillors were less critical than worker councillors on a number of issues: the effectiveness of councils and their potential for cooperative action, and the extent of protection against victimization. Councils in private firms were judged, on the whole, less favourably on these issues. There was a markedly higher level of conflict between manager and worker councillors in private firms.[7]

Our assessment of the usefulness of the works councils based on the above mentioned study and interviews is that the councils have not been very effective vehicles for worker participation. Thus the alleged central linchpin of worker participation as provided for in the IRA does not seem to be successful at all. Workers look to the trade unions for representation with management.[8] Workers interviewed by Fincham and Zulu indicated that they were not aware of what was discussed in works councils as they were not consulted in the first place. This could be attributed to the emphasis on secrecy in IRA relating to discussions on financial and other matters involving the work place. This had an effect on isolating councils from workers.[9] If this was the case, then councils were even less of vehicles for working class participation in management decisions. Miners who were interviewed felt that their trade union was more representative than the council.[10] This raises again the issue of whether works councils were erected to take the place of trade unions or neutralize trade unions. In either case they have failed as we have seen and shall see below.

Another issue that kept asserting itself in the course of research was the extent of workers' participation under private enterprise in general as well as under state capitalism existing in Zambia. According to Ben Turok, Zambia's State capitalism had the following characteristics: *(a)* state ownership of all major enterprises accounting for the greater part of total investment; *(b)* a largely unplanned, competitive commodity market governed by profit-making; *(c)* a class structure in which workers and peasants are in a subordinate position; *(d)* an emergent quasi-bourgeoisie which straddles the public and private sectors of the economy and, acting in varying forms of collaboration with foreign capital, penetrates the commanding heights of the economy and political system, and *(e)* the continuity and persistence of the system which is ensured by the mediation of state power.[11] How far could the bureaucratic bourgeoisie controlling the state in Zambia allow workers' participation to go? There is evidence that the state in Zambia was persuaded by private capitalists as well as parastatal-based bourgeoisie to water down its far-reaching proposals on the role of the works councils.[12] Commercial farmers persuaded the state to raise the number of employees from 25 to 100 in an enterprise that is eligible to set up a works council. The state agreed. Thus there are no works councils in commercial agriculture. Further, private capital impressed on the state that if private investment was to be forthcoming it needed to be clarified to what extent it would operate within the constraint of workers' participation. The private businessmen stated that "a very large number of the Zambian workers would not be able to understand the decisions of firms in which they were asked to participate. In the interests of all, the management of undertakings, whether private or parastatal must remain in competent hands."[13] The labour movement reacted sharply to the Businessmen's assessment of the Zambian worker, "... [this is] a bid to protect their capitalistic tendencies.... knowing very well that by giving power to their workers to participate in decision making, the businessmen feared losing their capitalistic extravangancies (posh cars, travelling allowance) they enjoyed which the workers, as co-workers of an enterprise would not approve of at a board meeting."[14] The state listened to management and quietly agreed. Thus what seems to exist as far as works councils go in Zambia, are watered down versions of workers' participation, the kind of councils that are consonant with private capitalism as well as state capitalism both of which are coexisting in Zambia. Workers have also seen that works councils do not go far enough, they are seen as vehicles of management and the state to neutralize industrial conflict in the latter twos' favour. Strong trade unions are seen by workers as representing more their interests. The inevitable conclusion is, "the value of councils as propaganda instruments, considering the secrecy of their proceedings, must be virtually nil, and as a channel of communication and influence over workers the councils have little potency".[15]

State evaluation of the effectiveness of works councils from the state's point of view shows that the state would like more to be achieved:

> Works councils are established in all undertakings employing not less than 100 eligible employees and the principal objective is to motivate employees to identify themselves more closely with the undertakings in which they work by fully participating in the decision-making process to foster harmonious industrial relations and higher productivity. The councils have mandate to be consulted and take part in decisions by managements relating to financial, economic and personnel policies. ... The operations of the councils established so far are reasonably effective. However a lot has to done in order for the councils to take hold of the task bestowed on them and in particular for employers to appreciate the role of the councils.[16]

At least the real aims (and not couched as in the (IRA) of councils are stated clearly as "to motivate employees" (not employer councillors), "to foster harmonious industrial relations and higher productivity". In the 1982 and 1983 reports of the Ministry of Labour and Social Services, the Works Councils were evaluated thus:

> Works councils established so far continued to function reasonably well. Seminars and training sessions for councillors continued to be the major preoccupation of trade unions and employers' associations. This is necessary in order to enable the Councillors to effectively perform the duties for which councillors were established ... During the year under review (1983) Councils contributed significantly in the maintenance of industrial tranquillity. However, for various reasons employers continued to thwart the effectiveness of Councils and in some incidences arbitrarily interfered with the smooth functioning of the Councils. In spite of lack of appreciation by some employers, Councils proved, in concerted effort with the trade unions to be an effective tool for harmonising industrial relations at the work places. Incidences of stoppages of work were curtailed.[17]

The issue of the education of Works Councils Councillors clearly indicate that much more was desired of these Councils and that participation had not yet been realised. It was still being prepared for. In the meantime, management which had not yet appreciated the work of the Councils was not being educated to appreciate the role of the Councils. Could it be that Management already knew what it wanted and expected out of the Councils and it was the Councils (mainly workers representatives) who must be educated to fulfil the "proper" role?

There is an indication in the 1983 report that the Councils, Trade Unions and the state expected the same thing from Councils and that it was the employers who were uncooperative. Our research however indicates that the state expected one thing and the trade unions expected another thing. The employers expect tame works councils, so does the state.[18] Until all the parties work for and expect the same thing out of the Councils, they will be deemed to be a failure. This is because they will be working at cross purposes. Or they may merely be rubber stamps of the policies of the dominant interests in which case the weaker entity will not be benefitting at all. This would be a failure (in the eyes of the weaker party) of the Works Councils.

Strikes

We belaboured the point in chapter 6 that the provisions of the IRA tended to rule out working class struggles in the form of strikes – legal or illegal. The question of the existence or not of strikes after the IRA came into operation is one of the strongest indicators of the success or failure of the IRA – that is, the failure of this instrument of class struggle waged by the bureaucratic bourgeoisie against the working class. We now set about analyzing the class struggles of the working class through the weapon of the strike. The year of departure for analysis is 1976.

In previous chapters it was made clear that the miners were wage setters in Zambia. It was also made clear that after each hefty wage award, strikes dwindled during that year and the following. During 1976, the agreement governing wages and salaries of the employees of the mining industry came up for review. As a result of negotiations which commenced well in advance, increases ranging up to 15 percent were awarded.[19] Because of this, a miners' strike was averted. Wage settlements were also concluded in parastatal organizations e.g. the Post and Telecommunications Department and in several companies in the private sector. As a result of these wage awards, 1976 was relatively quiet as far as working class struggles over wages were concerned.

Compared to the Sixties and early Seventies, 1977 was also relatively quiet as far as working class struggles were concerned. The wage awards of 1976 were still helping out somewhat to blunt the edge of the increasing cost of living. There were only 49 industrial strikes involving a loss of only 15,383 man-days,[20] perhaps one of the lowest man-days lost to strikes in the seventies.

In 1978 class struggles waged by the working class picked up in earnest. Forty-five strikes involving 41,320 workers and causing a loss of 296,727 man-days, one of the highest man-days lost recorded in the seventies occurred from January to September, 1978. Seventeen of these strikes occurred in the manufacturing industry.[21] Council workers in major towns also came out on strike increasing the labour unrest scene. After several years' quiet on the railways front, the railway workers also came out on strike which lasted for more than a week and paralysed travel in the rest of the country.

What was most interesting about these class struggles was that they were not mainly over wages, the supposedly usual concern of the working class. Out of the 45 strikes, only 16 strikes occurred because of wage demands, 21 strikes occurred over other issues e.g. conditions of employment etc. and 8 strikes occurred over collective agreements.[22] Thus strikes were still possible after the restrictions embodied in the IRA Almost all if not all of these strikes were wild-cat strikes. This means the IRA procedures were not followed.

These strikes also showed that not only the miners, the most heavily studied section of the Zambian working class, were capable of sponsoring major struggles. Further it showed that the public sector i.e. government and parastatal sectors were not immune from strikes. This also establishes the existence of class struggle between the working class and the bureaucratic bourgeoisie in Zambia since most strikes occurred in state parastatals.

In 1979, the number of strikes, workers on strike and man-days lost came down from those of 1978. The relevant data is contained in Table 7.5. According to the *Economic Report for 1979*,[23] strikes occurred as a result of a general rise in the cost of living and inadequate rise in wages allowed by employers in various sectors of the economy. An ILO expert, a Professor Turner,[24] who had prepared a report on incomes, wages and prices a decade previously, was commissioned again to do another study on the same theme in 1978. In the interim there had been other commissions on the same theme but nothing solid had been decided by the state. After the publication of the Turner Report, the government announced a general wage increase of K131 per annum. Workers in all sectors of the economy protested against this amount which was regarded as too small and the government was forced to raise the figure to K156 per annum. This clearly showed the political clout of the Zambian working class to force the state to back down on its previously announced wage policy.

This rarely happens in Zambia. It also showed the weakness of the state, that whenever it came into a very serious confrontation with the working class head to head, it backed down. It further showed the irresoluteness of the state – after so many commissions as well as the two Turner reports on incomes, salaries, wages and prices policy, the state had not settled on any one policy. This clearly shows muddle-headedness on the part of the bureaucratic bourgeoisie controlling the Zambian State. Even the state's legal armour embodied

Table 7.5

Monthly Summary of Strikes According to Economic Year 1979:

Month: January - September

Economic Activity According to ISIC	No. of Strikes	Workers Involved	No. of Man-Days Lost	No. of Wages Demands	Collective Agreements	Other Issues
Agriculture, hunting, forestry and fishing	6	2,799	6,993	5	-	1
Mining and quarrying	5	1,581	5,238	1	1	3
Manufacuturing	9	1,767	5,344	5	-	4
Electricity, gas and water	-	-	-	-	-	-
Construction	3	350	127	2	-	1
Wholesale and retail trade, restaurants and hotels	1	60	34	-	-	1
Transport, storage and communications	4	2,790	24,280	4	-	-
Finance, insurance, real estate and business services	1	31	8	-	-	1
Nongovernment business	-	-	-	-	-	-
Government services	1	21	63	-	-	1
Total	30	9,399	2,087	17	1	12

Source: *Annual Economic Report*, 1979, p. 33.

in the IRA to prevent strikes etc. was not used or was of no help in deciding
on clear policies that needed implementing. With lack of clear policy on the
part of the bureaucratic bourgeoisie, the working class easily scored on their
demands. The 1979 working class struggles further showed that the working
class was not always mainly interested in bread and butter issues e.g. wages
as the labour aristocracy thesis holds, but with other issues as well. Thus of
the 30 strikes in 1979, 17 of these were wage demands and 12 concerned other
issues, with 1 concerning a collective agreement. The miners even went on
strike more on other issues than on wages, 3 and 1 respectively. The working
class in manufacturing also showed themselves to be an increasingly militant
section of the working class, sponsoring 9 strikes, followed by agricultural
workers with 6 and miners with 5. It has also been pointed out that in 1978,
the workers in the manufacturing sector came out on more strikes than any
other section of the working class.

The Economic Report for 1980[25] saw 1980 as a good year to summarize
the state of industrial relations in Zambia for the previous decade. It was the
end of one decade and the start of another, thus a proper year to take stock.
The Report summarized:

> Generally speaking, the last decade witnessed increasing strike activity in
> Zambia although the situation was not as bad as that experienced between
> 1965 and 1969, both in terms of workers directly involved and man-days
> lost. The Post-Independence strike wave appears to have levelled off by
> 1970, in which year more man-days were lost compared to the previous
> three years ... Between 1971 and 1977, the country experienced relative
> industrial peace. The number of man-days lost did not exceed 40,000 per
> year, but the trend was broken in 1975 when 78 strikes led to a loss of
> 51,000 man-days. In 1978, however, 56 strikes involving 43,000 workers
> led to a loss of 301,600 man-days. The number of both strikes and
> man-days lost fell in 1979. The year 1980 has   witnessed an increase in
> the number of strikes to 93 which involved 21,821 workers resulting in
> 47,444 man-days lost ... wage demands have been the centre of most of
> these strikes. After the publication of the Turner Report, labour unrest
> broke out on a large-scale as each union tried to negotiate new scales of
> pay for their membership.[26]

Table 7.6 summarizes industrial disputes over the period 1970 – 1980.

The Labour Movement also summed up the developments in industrial
relations in the 1970s. "Fellow workers, we have come a long way: we have
worked under some very difficult and trying conditions and many times even
being suspected of political infidelity and pitied one against another by some
people whose intentions have clearly been to divide union leadership from

Table 7.6

Industrial Disputes Involving Loss of Work, 1970-1980

Year	No. of Disputes Reported	No. of Workers Directly Involved	No. of Man-days Lost
1970	12	32,300	123,000
1971	127	15,000	18,900
1972	74	10,500	20,900
1973	65	7,000	5,700
1974	55	7,400	38,700
1975	78	17,000	51,000
1976	59	5,600	6,500
1977	51	10,700	15,900
1978	56	43,100	301,600
1979*	30	10,500	42,100
1980*	93	21,800	47,400

*Expect for 1980 which covers the period from January – September, earlier years covered January – October.[27]

Source: Economic Report 1980 p. 52. This table clearly supports the State's analysis of industrial relations in the 1970 – 1980 period.

membership so as to cause rapture of confidence and trust which members have in us"[28] is the way F. Chiluba, Chairman-General of ZCTU opened his summing up of the developments in the 1970s. In politics, he took note of the close association with UNIP while preserving worker autonomy. In economics he pointed out that the general poor performance of the economy led to loss of employment for workers, drop in employment and standard of living, stagnation and decline in personal income, price escalation of goods and services but above all, curtailment of the freedom to bargain.

Chiluba also reported of some major differences with the government regarding industrial disputes. He mentioned the protracted case of railway workers (Tanzania and Zambia Railway (TAZARA)) who were dismissed.

There was also a "camouflaged" handling of salary and benefit increases for expatriate miners. Further he mentioned that "there was imposed a phoney overall wage of K131.00 per year which was subsequently altered to K156.00".

Chiluba also highlighted some notable successes of the labour movement: (a) Workers were better informed about their rights and responsibilities through seminars, workshops and press releases, (b) The labour movement itself was better known and understood than ever before, (c) The labour movement initiated the call for the legislation of maternity leave with pay for all women workers, (d) It also proposed the introduction of comprehensive social security scheme and (e) Demanded the establishment of a poverty datum line.

Chiluba promised more struggle for the 1980s. He said, "the 1980s must be so programmed as to close the communication gaps between workers and their unions and leaders so that any Mobilisation for action will be swift, almost spontaneous and effective. Our programmes at National union level and all their levels as well as the ZCTU should concentrate on measures which will consolidate trade unionism". The Labour Movement was poised to fight for the following in the 1980s, according to Chiluba:

> The immediate establishment of the minimum basic needs standards; opposition to any price increases which are not related to incomes; demands for full and productive employment creation; demand for job security based on accepted norms everywhere without tribe, clan, province, or political beliefs forming any criteria; demand for a comprehensive social security scheme; demand for a price freeze; demand for a speedier more effective and efficient Zambianization; demand for an immediate stop to employing aliens etc.

This was the programme for the 1980s.

If 1978 was the worst year in the seventies in terms of strikes, the worst was still awaiting the state. And if the strikes of the seventies were mainly about wages i.e. they were economic class struggles, the beginning of the eighties saw the movement towards political class struggles as well. Political class struggles in simple terms refer to situations whereby the working class through the unions take up broader political causes rather than being mainly concerned with narrowly defined economic issues. The movement towards political class struggles is what we turn our attention to now.

From Economic to Political Class Struggles

The working class struggles documented above have been abstracted from the political and economic conjuncture Zambia was experiencing at the time. But to properly understand the movement from economic to political class struggles, it is necessary to delve briefly into the political and economic context in which these class struggles were being waged.

Starting from the mid-seventies, Zambia experienced severe economic crisis, like most African countries. Due to sluggish demand for Copper (on which Zambia depends for foreign exchange earnings) on the world market, its price went down adversely affecting the economic viability to Zambia. At the same time as the copper prices went down, import prices soared. As a result, Zambia's "terms of trade" went down from 100 in 1970 to 35 in 1978, 50 in 1979 and 31 in 1981. This led to severe cutback on imports needed for industrial production, i.e. machines, spare parts, raw materials as well as consumer goods, and to serious shortages which in turn, together with the higher cost of imports, increased inflation within the country.[29] The prices of essential commodities, indeed all commodities soared up, adversely affecting consumers especially the unemployed and low wage workers. It was in response to the high cost of living that the massive strikes of 1978 were organized. The situation did not improve at all for the workers despite the wage increases. The time of economic crisis should be the time to have clear-cut policies on wages etc. But the State in Zambia was caught up in a contradiction. With the prices of consumer goods up, because of shortages etc., it could not justify lower wages of the workers. And the workers were in no mood for any wage restraints. Thus the state realised it was not the time to impose wage restraints stringently. There was also an election in 1978. The bureaucratic bourgeoisie did not want to unnecessarily antagonise the majority of the voting population i.e. the working class. Interviews I carried out revealed that the state bourgeoisie were cognizant of the dilemma it was in and decided the best policy, as always in Zambia, was to drift along and try to ride the waves hoping for calmer shores.

To make matters worse, despite the economic crisis Zambia was experiencing, the state bourgeoisie were living conspicuously rich. While the workers were being told daily in the *Zambia Daily Mail* and *Times of Zambia* to tighten their belts, the bourgeoisie were "loosening" theirs. The workers were justified in refusing to tighten their belts further. Jack Woddis captures the workers' mood beautifully under such conditions when he states that "if the working people could see a purpose of their having to go short of benefits for a time, if they felt it necessary to sacrifice now in order to put their country on its feet and lay the basis for prosperity in the future, they would probably be prepared to tolerate their difficulties. But in most African states they see on everyside waste and extravagance, corruption, bribery and embezzlement, nepotism and selfish careerism".[30] This applied fully to Zambia.

As Zambia entered the 1980s, there were grave economic crises in the country. With the onset of another round of economic crisis in the world economy at the end of the seventies, Zambia was bracing itself for worse times. The economic crises inevitably spilled into the political arena generating political crisis in the country. The response of the labour movement became more and more political. And so was the response of some sections of the bureaucratic, national, comprador and petty bourgeoisie. We start with the response of sections of the bourgeoisie.

The opening shot was fired in April 1980 by Elias Chipimo, Chairman of the Standard Bank Zambia (Ltd.), a foreign affiliate, when he publicly expressed the view that the "multi-party system was the surest way of avoiding coups and eliminating the disgraceful tendency of presidents ending up with bullets in their heads".[31] The President responded at some length, stating that: "dissidents led by former Cabinet Ministers are behind a plot to incite the army into overthrowing the Government and to assassinate me".[32] Dr. Kaunda named the dissidents as Elias Chipimo, Valentine Musakanya (a former Minister for Technical Education and Vocational Training and Governor of the Bank of Zambia) and Andrew Kashita (former Minister of Mines and Industry). Others implicated in "this vicious and deliberate campaign against the party and its Government" were Barclays Bank Zambia Manager Francis Nkhoma, and former Minister of Education and Finance John Mwanakatwe. Several months later on October 16, an attempted Military Coup was nipped in the bud. Within a week of the attempted coup, seven prominent Zambians were arrested: Chipimo, Musakanya, Patrick Chisanga, Edward Shamwana (a lawyer, former High Court Commissioner and Manager of ITT) as well as three senior army officers. They were all detained under emergency powers regulations. They were eventually charged in 1981, the trial dragged on until 1983 when eventually six were found guilty and sentenced to death.[33] No one was ever executed and eventually all of them were released, some as late as 1990.

The disaffection between the state based bourgeoisie and the other fractions of the bourgeoisie was essentially over the economic direction the country was headed under the leadership of the state bourgeoisie. The economy was in a shambles. There were no new directions or programmes proposed by the state to correct the situation. This is what precipitated the political crisis mentioned above.

It was the same with the labour movement. ZCTU was convinced that the state had consistently failed to respond to workers' demands to improve their standard of living. A political confrontation with the state was inevitable. We now turn to examining the political crisis that ensured.

Before the attempted coup, the labour movement opened fire. In September 1980, ZCTU Chairman Frederick Chiluba announced that "industrial workers had to brace themselves for industrial action" and that he was "ready to press the button at any time for a national strike before the end of the year". "It is time for us all to unite", he urged, "and be prepared to die". Denouncing the high crime rate, deteriorating economic conditions and the privileged lifestyle of the elite, Chiluba added that "we must be prepared to suffer, to be prosecuted and to be jailed to bring about improvements".[34] The labour movement had now entered political waters. The government perceived the strike threat as politically motivated. And sure it was, despite numerous statements by labour leaders that their interests were not political but to further the economic interests of the workers. As Chiluba, Chairman-General of ZCTU has stated, "the Labour Movement is not an alternative to government. In this context I want to state that the ZCTU is not the alternative to the government of the Republic of Zambia so that if the latter fails to achieve the goals of its plans it should not cast its eyes on the former as if we caused the evaporation of jobs in the country".[35] Chiluba has also defined several times the role of trade unions:

> We rededicate ourselves to the cause of free and democratic trade union-ism. We must commit ourselves as always to the fight for political, economic and social justice ... We must learn to defend at all costs the work of trade unions in this country and to this end we must oppose and fight all designs aimed at maiming the work and structure of the labour movement.[36]

The political context of this fight was however not being forgotten:

> And this [the aims in above quote] is not easy to achieve if we do not get to the roots of the matter − which is the government.[37]

Thus economic struggles existed in a political context which meant the labour movement inevitably had to tread into political waters. This they realised:

> Modern trade unionism cannot be restricted to begging or asking for wages and working conditions only which in any case never get better ...[38]

> [However] when a citizen cries for a fair share of the national wealth don't look at it as a political motive but a citizen's right ...[39]

Workers of Zambia must stand firm and resolve to restore order. Time has come for all of us who care for the future of this land to face realities. We will be prosecuted. We must suffer now. We must be jailed if necessary.[40]

This undoubtedly exhibits political consciousness on the part of the labour movement, at least of their leaders in Zambia. The leaders had began to articulate clearly political statements. This same year, the labour movement for the first time openly opposed what the government termed as a "political reform" move. The government came up with a Bill called Local Government Administration Bill which ostensibly called for more effective decentralization of power. Since the Bill provided for the standing and participation in local elections of UNIP members only, and this literally meant only active and visible UNIP notables, the labour movement thought this Bill would take away voting rights of its membership, thus reducing its power and increasing that of UNIP. The labour movement did not buy the alleged reason for decentraliza-tion i.e. to democratise the political system. The labour movement asked: How could the government democratise and decentralise power when an elected Mayor was now replaced by an appointed Mayor? Previously a Mayor of a district or rural council was a direct representative of the people who elected him, but, now democracy had been curtailed and power became more central-ized. In other words the decentralization move was suspicious. There was also an economic reason for the labour movement's opposition to the Bill. The new system would require paying more than K500,000 a month in salaries and allowances to 20 more councillors and local administrators in each district.[41] Given the disastrous economic situation the country was experiencing, the labour movement felt the paying of those salaries were an unnecessary ex-pense. Nevertheless, despite heavy opposition from the labour movement, the decentralization Bill was passed by parliament in December 1980 as *Local Administration Act* (1980) and came into effect on 1st January, 1981.[42] As it soon became evident, the government would not bear the expense of running a costly local government system, neither would the local councils. True to form however, the system was in a shambles by 1985. The councils were in debt, local facilities had collapsed and the government could ill afford to pump millions of dollars into the system.[43] Throughout the eighties and early nine-ties, the bankruptcy of councils made headlines and political leaders started urging people to sue the councils. In the early eighties the political leadership would not heed the warnings of the labour leaders.

The passage of the *Local Administration Act* (1980) was to strain relations between the state and the labour movement to almost breaking point in the course of 1981. At its Bi-annual Conference in 1980, MUZ resolved to boycott the elections that were to usher in the new system and further to expel from the Union any of their members who participated in the elections. This resolution was supported by ZCTU which went further to order all other affiliated trade unions not to participate in any way in the operations of the new system. Needless to say, the state regarded this as a challenge to its authority. The party retaliated swiftly against ZCTU and MUZ leaders. On January 16, 1981 the party Central Committee expelled from UNIP, Chiluba (ZCTU Chairman-General), Newstead Zimba (ZCTU Secretary-General and member of Parliament), Sampa (ZCTU Deputy Secretary-General), David Mwila (MUZ Chairman) and 13 other ZCTU and MUZ leaders.[44]

The labour movement also reacted quickly against the state for expelling the labour leaders from UNIP. For a while it was not clear whether the labour leaders were also expelled from their union positions. Zimba had to vacate his parliamentary seat. On January 20, 1981, more than 50,000 miners of the MUZ starting from Nchanga Consolidated Copper Mines (NCCM) went on strike in protest. The strike soon spread to Mufulira, Chibuluma, Chambeshi, Ndola Copper Refinery and Rokana Mines. These strikes were of course wild-cat and "illegal". The IRA procedures were not followed. They were not even in furtherance of a collective dispute. The government called the strikes an attempt at a coup plot.[45] On January 22, 1981, two days after the miners' strike commenced, Bank and Zambia State Insurance Company clerks also went on strike in five major towns which paralysed the financial system in the country. Although the workers in the financial sector went on strike concerning other conditions than the expulsion of the country's labour leaders from UNIP, nevertheless they could not have called the strike at a particularly bad time for the state. Teachers on the Copperbelt, members of the Zambia Electricity Workers Union at Ndola, and Postal Workers at Lusaka, Ndola and Kitwe briefly went on sympathetic strikes for the miners and workers in financial institutions. This labour solidarity was quite refreshing. The IRA was again shown to be impotent.

The miners went back to work after 8 days' strike and after assurances from the Minister of Labour and Social Services that the labour leaders expelled from UNIP would continue to hold their leadership positions in the respective unions. The strike cost Zambia about K20 million in foreign exchange earnings.[46] This short miners' strike also accounted for the total loss of about 123,256 man-days. In April 1981, the labour leadership was reinstated in UNIP.

The troubles between the state and the labour movement did not end after the reinstatement of the Labour leaders into UNIP. In early July, 1981, over 700 railway workers went on an "illegal" and wild-cat strike protesting against government-imposed managerial changes at Zambia Railways. The strike paralysed all rail traffic. Rail Transport is the most important means of transport in Zambia and is one of those facilities listed as essential services in the IRA As usual the government regarded that strike as politically motivated.

The railway workers' strike was soon joined by 10,000 mineworkers at Konkola division of NCCM who went on strike to protest against a decision by company management to halt company supplied emergency food allocation. The strike only lasted 7 days during which time management and union officials agreed to critically examine the problems and to appoint an agency to distribute mealie-meal to the miners. On July 17, 1981, Mineworkers at Luanshya and Kabwe staged another major strike in support of Zambian graduate skilled workers who were demanding large wage increases to narrow the gap between themselves and 3,000 expatriates employed in the mines. (There was still a pay disparity between locals and expatriates. There still is). David Mwila, Chairman of MUZ declared that "these strikes are symptoms of the people's growing disenchantment with this government's economic policies". This strike which lasted over a week accounted for the loss of 118,538 man-days and millions of Kwacha in Copper revenue. Management and MUZ resolved to smooth the income inequalities.

The spate of strikes obviously further shook an already politically shaken government. Thus on July 27, 1981, the president invoking emergency powers to ostensibly "preserve" public security, detained Chiluba (ZCTU Chairman-General), Zimba (ZCTU Secretary-General), Sampa (ZCTU Deputy Secretary-General) and Timothy Walamba (MUZ Vice-Chairman). Kaunda declared that the "ZCTU leaders were exploiting the economic problems for their political ends". According to Kaunda, the labour leaders were instigating illegal strikes with the aim of toppling the party leadership. He was also concerned with the increase in the number of such strikes (84 illegal strikes by July, 1981) which had already by mid-year involved over 46,000 workers, more than double those involved in the whole of 1980. And the labour leaders were increasingly articulating political sentiments rather than the bread and butter issues of concern to the Zambian working class. Kaunda had not used emergency powers to detain labour leaders for 10 or more years thus the 1981 detentions were regarded as a "move which marks the country's most serious political crisis since independence"[47] as far as labour-state relations were concerned. There were discussions in ZCTU to call for a general strike to protest against the detention of ZCTU and MUZ leaders, but such a move was not endorsed. Instead ZCTU appealed to the president to release the labour leaders. The labour leaders challenged the detention orders in the High Court of Zambia. They had been detained for allegedly instigating illegal strikes which were aimed at toppling the government. The Court however found that: "the cause of the first strike (of January 20, 1981) was the expulsion of the 17 labour leaders (from UNIP); the withdrawal of the mealie meal credit facility and the demand for equal pay by the Zambian graduates and artisans, were the causes of the second (July 7, 1981) and (July 17, 1981) strikes respectively",[48] and were thus not instigated by the labour leaders. Regarding the invocation of the *Preservation of Public Security Act*, the Court had this to say:

> Coming to the statement that ... labour leaders were intent at taking over the country's leadership, it does not state the means by which they were and/or still are to achieve their desired goal. Simply to express an ambition to take over the leadership of the country perse does not make the author of that statement a public security risk. He must be a threat to the politicians in their political jobs, but that is an area of activity which is totally different from public security matters. Unless it is shown that the fulfilment of political ambitions touches on public security and its preservation, people must be allowed to aspire to the highest offices in the land. It would not be proper to react to political threats from certain individuals by having recourse to the provisions of the *Preservation of Public Security Act* and detaining people thereunder when the matters on which they would be detained had nothing to do with Public Security and its preservation.[49]

Consequently the Court found that the state's case had no basis and thus the detentions were revoked and the labour leaders were released in November 1981. Normally the President would simply have redetained the individuals and issued new detention orders. But he saw fit not to do that in this case. The atmosphere in the labour movement was charged and probably feared that there would be another round of destructive strikes.

Thus 1981 was the most explosive year as far as class struggles between the state and the labour movement were concerned. There were in all 156 strikes involving 76,776 workers resulting in a loss of 556,408 man-days. These figures indicate an increase compared to the strikes which took place in 1980 which were recorded at 121 involving 28,434 workers and causing a loss of 79,896 man-days.[50] As Table 7.7 shows the workers' struggles were not limited to wage demands only. The overwhelming number of strikes were concerned with other issues i.e. political questions or conditions of employment etc. (66.7%) while 23.7% were concerned with wage demands and 9.6% with collective agreements. This was in fact a trend already established in previous years by the labour movement in Zambia.

The labour movement scored impressive victories in 1981. There was a successful strike against the expulsion of labour leaders from UNIP. Solidarity within the labour movement was underscored when many unions went on sympathetic strikes in support of MUZ which was spearheading the protest against the expulsion of the labour leaders. The labour leaders were reinstated into UNIP. The railway workers successfully resisted government imposed management changes. The miners also successfully resisted management re-

Table 7.7
Strikes, 1981

Economic Activity According to ISIC	No. of Strikes	No. of Workers Involved	No. of Man-Days Lost	Wages Demand		No. of Strikes over			
						Collective Agreements		Other Issues	
				No.	Man-Days	No.	Man-Days	No.	Man-Days
Agriculture, hunting, forestry and fishing	6	1,783	1,282	4	1,737	-	-	2	455
Mining and quarrying	30	60,223	517,635	14	124,730	-	-	16	392,905
Manufacuturing	16	1,586	10,680	6	8,946	3	945	7	789
Electricity, gas and water	1	400	215	-	-	-	-	1	215
Construction	19	4,794	9,291	7	809	11	8,442	1	40
Wholesale and retail trade, restaurants and hotels	2	200	344	1	324	1	-	1	20
Transport, storage and communications	8	2,031	2,472	3	1,269	-	477	4	726
Finance, Insurance, real Estate and business services	66	5,449	13,010	-	-	-	-	66	13,010
Nongovernment business	6	11	53	-	-	-	-	2	53
Government services	2	299	971	2	415	-	-	4	556
Total	156	76,776	556,408	37	137,775	15	9,864	104	408,769
				23.7%	24.8%	9.6%	1.8%	66.7%	73.4%

Source: *Annual Report, 1981,* Ministry of Labour and Social Services

moval of the mealie-meal credit system. Zambian graduate miners also forced the management to examine incomes disparities between them and expatriate workers. Finally the labour movement successfully challenged, using the courts, the state's emergency powers under which ZCTU and MUZ leaders were detained by the president following the July 1981 strikes.

Was this trajectory of class struggle to continue in 1982? Compared to 1981, 1982 was relatively quiet as far as class struggles were concerned. There were only 39 strikes involving 4,056 workers and resulting in a loss of 7,702 man-days. The strikes were mainly caused by workers demanding wage increases as a result of the escalating cost of living in the country. As a result of the serious economic situation in the country, the government decontrolled prices of certain commodities. Immediately the prices of goods, particularly essential commodities went up. This brought a sharp reaction from the labour leaders who felt that the lowly paid workers would suffer as they could not afford the new prices. The labour leaders had by now established themselves as spokesmen for the working class and ordinary citizens. As in all previous years, the strikes were "illegal" as well as "unconstitutional" as laid down procedures in the IRA were not followed.[51] The government did not resort to the provisions of the IRA to deal with illegal strikes, instead it simply terminated the employment of those workers identified as ring leaders.

Nineteen eighty three can be called the year of the battle over wages. In January 1983, the government announced that increases in wages and salaries would be limited to ten percent. The Turner Report of 1978 had recommended a three-phase process of regulating prices and incomes. The first two phases had placed restrictions on wage rises. In 1981, the president announced that phase three would commence in August 1982, whereby there would be a removal of restriction in wage rises. Trade unions and employers were free to agree on any amount of increases, the only constraint being the ability of the employer to pay. There was to be established a Prices and Incomes Commission as recommended by the Turner Report in 1978 to investigate and recommend long term guidelines for government action in the field of incomes, wages and prices. The Prices and Incomes Commission came into existence in 1981, but by 1983 it had not made any recommendations. Thus the President's direction that increases in wages and salaries would be limited to ten percent, without the recommendation of the Prices and Incomes Commission, was greeted negatively by the labour movement. And phase three of free collective bargaining was short-lived, hardly existing for six months.

The restriction on wage increases to ten percent received a sharp reaction from the labour movement who questioned the wisdom of restraining an upward movement of wages while prices of essential commodities were all allowed to escalate. In reaction to this, an unprecedented spate of wild-cat strikes commenced, demanding high wages. As can be seen from Table 7.8 and compared to other years, 1983 was the only year in a long time when most of the strikes were geared to wage demands (96.3%) as opposed to a mere 3.7% for other issues. There were economic reasons for this.

The president was forced to meet the labour leaders during the year whereby it was agreed that the wages and salaries ceiling would be maintained until 30 April, 1984, thereafter the position would revert to free collective bargaining.[52] This meeting signalled the growing strength of the labour movement, the ability to negotiate almost as equal power holders with the state bourgeoisie.

Decade of Disenchantment

Most labour leaders interviewed regarded the period from 1970 upwards as the most disagreeable in industrial relations in Zambia. The issues that stand out are; the use of detention against labour leaders by the president, the issue of decentralization; the party and government proposals to turn trade unions into mass organizations and government failure to establish a poverty datum line, among others.[53] As can be seen most of these issues are political and require political solutions.

This chapter has shown that the late seventies and early eighties saw unprecedented class struggles in Zambia. Workers resorted to illegal and wild-cat strikes. The labour leaders widened their concerns to include the articulation of political and economic issues affecting the whole country and not only limited to issues affecting the working class.

The workers totally disregarded the stipulations of the IRA regarding collective disputes and strike policy. As Table 7.9 shows, instead of bringing collective disputes to the IRC, the workers simply went on wild-cat strikes. The IRA was almost reduced to impotence.

What was also noticeable was the lack of resort to the IRA by the state regarding illegal and unconstitutional strikes. There were no prosecutions of illegal strikers. Neither were there any fines imposed against illegal strikers. Since the workers simply went on strikes without declaring a collective dispute, the IRC was reduced to approving collective agreements, recognition agreements, and receiving complaints and applications. One of its most important functions – to prevent strikes was aborted by the working class not obeying the dictates of the state and its laws.

Table 7.8
Stirkes, 1983

Economic Activity According to ISIC	No. of Strikes	No., of Workers Involved	No. of Man-Days Lost	Wages Demand		Collective Agreements		No. of Strikes over Other Issues	
				No.	Man-Days	No.	Man-Days	No.	Man-Days
Agriculture, hunting, forestry and fishing	3	338	226	3	226	-	-	-	-
Mining and quarrying	1	28	4	1	4	-	-	-	-
Manufacuturing	28	4,699	5,182	27	3,122	-	-	1	80
Electricity, gas and water	-	-	-	-	-	-	-	-	-
Construction	8	882	967	8	967	-	-	-	-
Wholesale and retail trade, restaurants and hotels	2	202	112	2	112	-	-	-	-
Transport, storage and communications	4	1,812	868	4	868	-	-	-	-
Finance, insurance, real Estate and business services	2	43	59	2	59	-	-	-	-
Nongovernment business	1	15	13	-	-	-	-	1	13
Government services	5	1,198	739	5	739	-	-	-	-
Total	54	9,217	8,170	52	8,097	-	-	2	73
				96.3%	99.1%	-	-	3.7%	0.9%

Source: *Annual Report, 1981,* Ministry of Labour and Social Services

Table 7.9

Activities of The Court

Year	Collective Agreement	Recognition Agreement	Compliant	Application	Appeals	Dispute	Total
1974	-	36	-	-	-	-	36
1975	22	54	3	-	2	2	81
1976	21	34	4	-	11	-	70
1977	18	10	5	-	2	-	35
1978	26	14	-	2	2	-	45
1979	31	19	28	94	2	2	176
1980	83	23	32	82	3	1	224
1981	97	18	60	93	3	1	172
1982	47	21	69	52	-	2	123
1983	29	30	68	22	2	2	153
1984	384	260	269	345	27	10	1,215

Source: *Annual Report, 1983*, Ministry of Labour and Social Services.

The next chapter discusses how the state responded to capture the initiative in dealing with the 'unruly' working class. I also discuss the broader theoretical and practical implications of the state and labour relations thrown up by the study of class struggles in Zambia. I continue that theme in the last chapters.

Notes

1. Republic of Zambia, Office of the Prime Minister. *Department of Industrial Participatory Democracy Report and Recommendations of the National Symposium On Industrial Democracy in Zambia Held at The President's Citizenship College, Mulungushi, 12-22 July 1976* (Lusaka: Government Printer, 1977).

2. Robin Fincham and Grace Zulu, "Labour and Participation in Zambia" in *Development in Zambia* edited by Ben Turok, (London: Zed Press, 1979) p. 217.

3. Ibid., p. 214 - 225.

4. Ibid., p. 217.

5. Ibid., p. 219.

6. Interviews, Lusaka and Kitwe, May 1985. See also *The Workers Voice*, Vol.3, No.2, September 1980, p. 7.

7. Fincham and Zulu, note 2, p. 221.

8. Interviews, Lusaka and Kitwe, May 1985.

9. Fincham and Zulu, p. 211.

10. Ibid.

11. Ben Turok, "Zambias System of state capitalism" *Development and Change*, Vol.11, 1980, p. 471.

12. Angela Quemby *"Works Councils and Industrial Relations in Zambia"* in Some Aspects of Zambian Labour Relations edited Evance Kalula, Lusaka: National Archives of Zambia, 1975, pp. 85-104. Fincham and Zulu, note 2, pp. 222-223. See also Tony Southall "Zambia: Class Formation and Government Policy in the 1970" *Journal of Southern African Studies*, Vol.7, No.1 (October 1980) pp. 93-108.

13. Quoted in "Workers' Participation" *The Workers Voice*, Vol.3, No.3 (October 1980) p. 10.

14. Ibid.

15. Fincham and Zulu, note 2, p. 224.

16. Republic of Zambia, Ministry of Labour and Social Services, *Annual Report for the Year 1981*, Lusaka: Government Printer, 1983, p. 15.

17. Ibid *Annual Report for the 1982 and 1983*, p. 7 and p. 8 respectively.

18. Interviews, Lusaka and Kitwe, May 1985. See also note 16.

19. Republic of Zambia. Ministry of Development Planning, *Economic Report 1976*. Lusaka, Government Printer, 1977, p. 94.

20. Republic of Zambia. Office of the Prime Minister. National Commission for Development Planning, *Economic Report 1978*, Lusaka: Government Printer, 1979, p. 106.

21. Ibid.

22. Ibid.

23. Republic of Zambia. Office of the President. National Commission for Development Planning, *Economic Report, 1979*, (Lusaka: Government Printer, 1980) p. 32.

24. Second Report to the Government of Zambia on Income, Wages and Prices in Zambia, I.L.O. Geneva 1978 (Turner Report).

25. Republic of Zambia. Office of the President, National Commission for Development Planning, *Economic Report, 1980*, (Lusaka: Government Printer, 1981).

26. Ibid., p. 51 and p. 52.

27. Some of the figures in this table differ from those quoted above in this chapter because the latter are for January-September, whereas the former are for January-October.

28. The Workers Voice, Vol.3, No. 1 (June 1980) p. 4. All further references are from this source.

29. See *Economic Reports 1975 - 1983* and Peter Meyns "The Political Economy in Zambia" in *Beyond Political Independence* edited by Klaas Woldring and Chibwe Chibaye, (Berlin et al.: Mouton, 1984) pp. 7-22.

30. Jack Woddis, *New Theories of Revolution*, (New York: International Publishers, 1974) p. 148.

31. *Times of Zambia*, 21 April, 1980.

32. *Times of Zambia*, 23 April, 1980.

33. See Munyonzwe Hamalengwa "The Politics of Detention in Zambia" Human Rights Internet Document, Washington, D.C. January 1983. See also "Zambia" in *Amnesty International Report 1983*, (London: Amnesty International, 1984) The sentence to date has not yet been carried out.

34. *Times of Zambia*, 29 September, 1980.

35. The Workers Voice, Vol.3, No.2 (September 1980) p. 2.

36. Speech given by Frederick Chiluba, Chairman-General of Zambia Congress of Trade Unions to Seminar members of ZCTU General Council at Kabwe, 28th September, 1980.

37. Ibid.

38. Ibid.

39. Editorial, *The Workers Voice*, Vol.3, No.3, October 1980, p. 6.

40. Note 32.

41. Times of Zambia, also pointed out in Klaas Woldring "Corruption and Inefficiency in Zambia – a Survey of Recent Inquiries and their results" *Africa Today*, Vol.30, No.3, 1983, pp. 70-71. The article is reprinted in *Beyond Political Independence in Zambia*, Note 28.

42. See National Institute of Public Administration, *Decentralization: A Guide to Integrated Local Administration*, Lusaka, August, 1981.

43. See *The Workers Voice*, Vol.2, No.18 (February 1985) p. 1 and *National Mirror*, No.229 (May 17 – May 30, 1985) pp. 6 and 8.

44. *Zambia Daily Mail* 17 January, 1981, *Keesings Contemporary Archives* February 27, 1981, p. 30738, November 13, 1981 p. 31185 and October 29, 1982 p. 31783; *Africa Confidential*, Vol.22, No.22, October 28, 1981, pp. 1-2.

45. *Times of Zambia*, 22 January, 1981.

46. Woldring, Note 41, p. 72.

47. The Financial Times Quoted in *Keesings Contemporary Archives*, November 13, 1981, p. 31186.

48. See *Re Walamba and Sampa* (High Court of Zambia, 1981) Reproduced in *Civil Liberties Cases in Zambia*, by Muna Nduland Kaye Turner, Oxford, 1984, pp. 294-304 and *Re Chiluba* pp. 304-324.

49. *Re Walamba and Sampa*, Ibid., pp. 300-1.

50. Ministry of Labour and Social Services, *Annual Report for the Year 1981*, Lusaka: Government Printer, 1983, p. 14.

51. Ministry of Labour and Social Services, *Annual Report for the Year 1982*, Lusaka: Government Printer, 1984, p. 5.

52. Ministry of Labour and Social Services, *Annual Report for the Year 1983*, Lusaka: Government Printer, 1985, p. 4.

53. Some of these are mentioned by J. Mubanga of the Railway Workers Union of Zambia (MUZ) (March 13, 1987).

8

The State Strikes Back:
1985 Onwards

According to Woldring, writing in 1983:

> the ZCTU has emerged as a viable *de facto* opposition party. Although in the main still concerned with working conditions and wages the ZCTU has increasingly pronounced on and often criticised general political matters. Reluctantly, the leaders of the political elite have accepted this new role. What remains to be seen of course is whether or not this new dimension of Zambian politics will provide the framework, within UNIP, for significant change.[1]

If the ruling party accepted the new role of the working class as an unofficial opposition, it sure did not appear that this new role was given a permanent status by the party. It was a temporary recognition of the shifts in power relations between the state and the working class, and temporary hiatus allowed while the state was readjusting for a counter-attack. In reality the state never ceased to try to weaken the working class.

The latest offensive aimed at striking a death blow to the labour movement came with *Statutory Instrument Number 6 of 1985*, known as *Trade Unions (Deduction of Subscription) Regulation 1985*. The purpose of the Instrument which was issued on January 19, 1985 was to revoke any prior orders given to employers to deduct union subscriptions from wages of employees where members of a trade union had gone on an illegal strike. The Instrument was brought about by the Minister of Labour and Social Services in terms of section 20 of the IRA which permits him to issue orders to employers to deduct union subscriptions and at the same time reserve him the power to revoke such orders.

This measure was taken as a result of a growing concern by the state on the proliferation of illegal strikes, mentioned in the previous chapter, in Zambian industries. These strikes were seen as a matter of indiscipline among union members who chose to go on strike in total disregard of procedures in the IRA for solving industrial disputes. Through the Instrument, the state hoped to punish erring unions and their members by depriving them of an effective and efficient mechanism of revenue collection to run their affairs. It follows that if the unions cannot run their affairs effectively, they will thus be weak and unable to offer resistance to the onslaught of the state. This may also be an incentive to unions and their members to abide by law relating to resolution of collective disputes rather than to go on illegal strikes. As already pointed out in chapter 6, if dispute resolution mechanisms enunciated in the IRA were followed to the letter, there would effectively have been no strikes in Zambia.

The Instrument immediately came to be used potently. Within six months of its coming into effect, it was slapped on the following unions for going on illegal strikes: National Union of Postal and Telecommunications Workers; Zambia Electricity Workers Union; Zambia Union of Financial Institutions and Allied Workers; Zambia National Union of Teachers and the Mineworkers Union of Zambia. Thus the state meant business to undercut the basis of the strength of the labour movement – its financial base.[2]

The labour movement of course condemned the coming into force of Instrument number 6 of 1985.[3] ZCTU also challenged the legality of the Instrument in Kitwe High Court. This legal challenge was however defeated. The High Court ruled on May 14, 1985 that the order by the Minister of Labour and Social Services was a legal exercise of his discretionary power given him by section 20(12) of the *Industrial Relations Act* and could not be a subject of question in a court of law. The state did not stop with Instrument Number 6, 1985 in its attempts to weaken the labour movement. Early in 1985 the Minister of Labour and Social Services introduced a Bill in Parliament in which he proposed amendments to the IRA which would have an effect of turning trade unions into "mass organisations", like UNIP's Youth and Women's Leagues. The labour movement vehemently condemned this move to turn trade unions into the ruling party's mass organizations. Addressing a trade union conference, Chiluba, ZCTU Chairman-General articulated the labour movement's opposition:

A trade union movement is a specialist workers' organization which only caters for people in formal employment with distinguishable employers working under prescribed laws... A trade union cannot be a mass organization because its membership is not open to everyone in the country ... like in a political party.[4]

Chiluba feared that the ruling party was turning into political absolutism:

> True to absolutism, the party wants to control absolutely the news media, the church, the trade unions and industry and even football and net ball so that every citizen will exist because of the party, instead of the party existing because of its members who are drawn from the country's citizens.[5]

The labour movement must not be seen as a threat to Zambian politicians, according to Chiluba:

> In fact the one-party system of politics in Zambia requires an independent free strong trade union movement to provide positive pressure to check on government excesses so as to ensure accountability of political leadership.[6]

He exalted the working class to fight on:

> Workers must resist any attempts at neutralizing and liquidating their free voice provided through the trade unions.[7]

In an editorial in the *Worker's Voice* for February 1985, the ZCTU identified 1985 as a watershed year in the history of the labour movement in Zambia due to the threat posed by Instrument Number 6 of 1985 and the Bill to turn trade unions into mass organizations, by stating that "1985 will be recorded in the annuals of Industrial Relations history in Zambia as the year the basic Trade Union Freedom died at the stroke of a pen overnight". The effect of turning trade unions into mass party organizations would be that they would be tightly controlled by UNIP and would receive instructions from UNIP. In other words, trade unions would be penetrated and rendered less effective to fight for the interests of the workers.

As for the effect of the removal of automatic deduction of union dues by employers, Beele envisaged this move to be a challenge to the trade union leadership to find effective ways of collecting dues from the members.[8] If this is successful, it would have the effect of strengthening union organisation and fostering independence and autonomy from employers and the state. If this is not successful, it would be a real test for trade unions in Zambia to continue operating and organizing.

Instrument No. 6, 1985 did not really address the cause of illegal strikes in Zambia. Firstly, the state has not made a case that trade unions are responsible for illegal strikes. Usually these strikes are started by the rank and file members and the trade union officials find that they have no choice but to support them, if they want to retain their leadership positions. Secondly, trade unions have pointed out that the procedure for obtaining legal strikes in Zambia is so cumbersome that a legal strike may never be, under the present legislation. Yet without threats of imminent strikes, few employers are moved to attend to employee grievances promptly. Thus inability to attain legal strikes coupled with lack of incentives on employers to attend to employee grievances in time, chokes the industrial relations system resulting in employee frustrations manifested in illegal strikes. Beele suggests that the long term solution would be for the state to cut down on the procedural requirements necessary to obtain legal strikes so that the threat of strikes could become meaningful economic weapons possessed by organised labour against employers.[9] A ZCTU symposium made the same point when it resolved that "... most industrial unrest in [Zambia] emanate from prolonged periods in the course of collective agreements ratifications". There is no need for further delays after such prolonged periods, thus, "the collective agreements once agreed upon by the two parties should be forwarded to the Industrial Relations Court for registration only"[10] and not for approval or disapproval which restarts the long process all over again.

The state has also not followed the stipulations of the IRA regarding illegal strikes. No remedial actions have ever been taken. Up to the second half of the 1980s, employees who had gone on strikes not authorised by a strike ballot as required by section 116(2) of the IRA had never been prosecuted as demanded by law. Section 116(4) of the IRA stipulates that the penalty for participating in an illegal strike is a jail term of six months or a fine of one hundred Kwacha or a combination of them. These deterrent provisions have been left as dead letters by the state.[11] Of course there are logistical problems in sending to prison or fining thousands of workers. The image of the state would be tarnished. However, in 1988 there was heightened talk about prosecuting teachers who went on illegal strikes. But the state has in the long run attempted to tame the labour movement by other means – to weaken the unions by financial starvation and firings. However the unions may be spurred to renew organizational activities and continue surviving. No union had been liquidated as a result of lack of funds by the end of 1985.

Muvoywa M. Kaiko, of the Zambia National Union of Teachers (ZNUT) reports however that in "1985 – 1986 union dues were reduced drastically due to the application of section 20 of the Industrial Relations Act. All union activities came to a standstill because of lack of funds".[12] According to M. K. Sumani of the Mineworkers Union of Zambia (MUZ), Statutory Instrument No. 6 of 1985 "was intended to weaken the labour movement [and this] resulting into conflicts between Trade Unions and the Government".[13] For example the National Union of Teachers went on a massive strike in the early part of 1987 as a result of this instrument.

Another tactic used by the government against illegal strikers, was firings. Timothy Walamba, Chairman of the Mineworkers Union of Zambia reports that MUZ members "who have gone on strikes after failing to go through the [lengthy] established channels have been labelled as illegal strikers and therefore most of them have lost their jobs through government directives".[15] According to Sumani of MUZ more than 3,000 members have lost their jobs as a result of the effects of Instrument No. 6 of 1985.[16] It is not easy at the moment to foresee the long term effects of this Instrument.

Workers in the Political Economy of Zambia

In the concluding chapter of his pioneering work, *The Story of an African Working Class: Ghanaian Miners' Struggles, 1970-1980*,[17] entitled "The Limits of Militancy: Mine Worker Resistance and Political Change in Ghana", Jeff Crisp asks a very crucial question which we rephrase to suit our study: To what extent can the [Zambian] workers' resistance be regarded as a force for progressive change within the [Zambian] political economy?"[18] Crisp finds that there have been serious limitations to Ghanaian Miners' Militancy. Firstly their militancy has not been expressed in class terms but in occupational terms. This lack of worker solidarity has meant that opportunities that existed to influence political developments were lost. Secondly Mine Workers in Ghana have traditionally displayed very little interest in participating in the national political arena. Given their strategic importance to the Ghanaian political economy, their participation would have had profound political impact. Thirdly, the mineworkers have never espoused any radical political ideology. They possess no vision of an alternative socio-political order. He then counterpoises the situation with Ghanaian railwaymen whom he calls 'radical populists' and "who share a coherent ideal of an open and responsive political system, who are committed to participation as an effective independent force in national politics, and who project themselves as the spokesmen of the masses, particularly the labouring poor".[19]

However, Crisp has not been too haste to dismiss the miners. Despite the fact that "throughout their long history of militant resistance the mineworkers have displayed very little interest in acting in alliance with other workers, in not having clearly defined political ideals and in remaining highly sceptical of the value of participation in the national political arena",[20] "the Mine Workers Union of Ghana ... cannot be dismissed as irrelevant to the Mine Workers' struggle against their exploitation, or indeed to the broader struggle for progressive change within the Ghanaian political economy".[21] To do otherwise would be to fall into structuralism whose limitations were exposed in chapter one. Casting the net wider, Crisp recognises that "in the unstable states of post-colonial Africa [trade unions] represent one of the few means whereby authoritarian and elitist regimes can be held in check, or even removed".[22] And this is good enough. Thus mine workers in Ghana despite their limitations have had positive progressive impact in Ghana.

What can be said of the Zambian working class as a whole as represented by their unions and the national umbrella organization – ZCTU? While the Zambian labour movement has no radical political ideology (which it is not in any case inexorably supposed to have), ZCTU and individual unions have been very active in organising the entire working class for pressure for progressive political and economic change in Zambia and have demanded vehemently for participation in the national political arena. Some of their resistances as well as demands have already been documented above and will not be repeated below except for emphasis.

While Zambian workers' interests and struggles can be regarded as economistic or mere trade unionism, it has to be understood that this has been part and parcel of class struggle to appropriate some of the surplus that would otherwise have gone to the ruling class or private and international capital. Union members have also pressed hard on their unions to deliver. Further the permanent economic crisis in Zambia, some of which has been due to falling Copper prices as already stated elsewhere and some of which has resulted from state mismanagement, has compelled workers to demand more "economistic" rewards. Walamba of MUZ has explained it this way, "... the social, economic and political policies introduced by the government brought about negative effects on the workers such as high taxes, restriction on wages, increased prices of goods as compared to poor services in schools, hospitals, housing and many others – this therefore entailed a lot of pressure on the unions from their members demanding for increased salaries to cushion off the above effects".[23] When labour leaders were asked in the Questionnaire what were the interests of the Zambian workers, the responses were typical: "Competitive salaries", "good housing", "good medicare", "Affordable goods and services" "good standard of living", "better and safe working conditions", "provision of all other social amenities", "Better and well equipped classrooms", "Better education", "funeral assistance", "Full participation in nation-building", "Attractive pension and life assurance schemes", "job security".

These are universal workers' demands and their fulfilment would be a definite contribution to progressive political, social and economic change. The labour movement has rejected the government charge that wage demands aggravate the already worsening economic situation. Chiluba, Chairman-General of ZCTU has put it this way, "any trade unionist who accepts not to ask for higher wages because they aggravate the situation but at the same time allows inadvertently or deliberately the wage gaps to continue must quit. That there are those yawning gaps in the country everyone accepts. But when we agitate for their bridging we then differ – I cannot understand".[24]

This clearly shows that the "economistic" demands of the Zambian workers is partly in order to redress the wage imbalances between the poor and the rich. According to Chiluba, "The incomes disparities in Zambia are such that salaries of ten people in the high income bracket can account for the incomes in wages of two hundred productive workers in the low income bracket".[25] The mine workers particularly feel robbed by the parastatal based bourgeoisie and workers in parastatal enterprises. Walamba explains that one of the most disagreeable aspects of the relationships between the government and MUZ is that:

> The union and its members feel cheated by the Government, in that the union operates in an industry which sustains the nation but its members are poorly rewarded compared to other workers in loss making parastatal organisations. In fact the policy to nationalise the [mining] industry means that all negotiable matters cannot be concluded with an employer without government intervention.[26]

The Zambian labour movement has been very consistent in criticising governmental, political and economic policies and which have earned them respect not only from union members but grudging notice from political leaders. The labour movement has also earned the notice and respect of the majority of Zambians for their consistency in progressive criticism of government. Indeed according to Chiluba, ZCTU is today a household name in Zambia. "Although some choose to mispronounce it deliberately because its work haunts them, those who accept and appreciate its value strive to call it by its proper name".[27] What a change compared to the pre-70s when ZCTU was despised! One of the economic policies the labour movement has consistently criticised is the wastage of resources in parastatal organisations. While the labour movement has criticised parastatal organizations, "the labour movement", according to John Sichone, then ZCTU acting Assistant Secretary-General for Organization and Administration, "is not against nationalization of private companies [or the creation of parastatals] but is concerned about the poor performance of these institutions".[28] The labour movement in Zambia is skeptical of parastatals after noting that within six months of their parastatalization in 1975, percentage of wastage in these institutions jumped up astronomically (see following figures).

In three years from 1975, local expenses in the above institutions increased by over 20 million Kwacha.[29] The situation has worsened since then.[30] The wastage in the parastatals was taken note of also at the symposium of the

INDECO MILLING COMPANY

Head office expenses jumped by	71%
Motor vehicle expenses increased by	144%
Salaries and wages	108%
Travelling	13%
Entertainment	167%
Advertising	2211%

COLD STORAGE BOARD OF ZAMBIA

Head office administration jumped by	25%
Loss in cattle department	294%

REFINED OIL PRODUCTS LIMITED

Sales fell by	K27,000
Interest and management fees increased by	65%
Salaries increased by	54%
Office administration by	111%
Travelling, distribution expenses increased by	176%

DAIRY PRODUCE BOARD

Sales of liquid milk and cream	10 or 11%
Travelling expenses increased by	159%
Advertising	139%
Wages and salaries	54%
Factory, marketing and other expenses	73%

labour movement in 1980. The redirection of public funds for private accumulation was also noted. "The symposium is appalled at the present careless
manner of public spending. The present system of accountability for public
funds is not effective thereby leaving the executive virtually free to spend
public funds on luxurious goods and services. This has led to the redirection
of funds earmarked for national development projects to pay for [private]
luxurious goods and services instead".[31]

The ruling class in Zambia has tried to show that working class criticism
of parastatals means the workers are in support of capitalism and in opposition
to socialism espoused by the State. Some state ideologists have also tried to
portray the labour movement as part of the right wing opposition.[32] The labour
movement has, however, countered that its aim is to expose corruption and
instill a sense of accountability and responsibility in the use of public funds.
The labour movement is also interested in efficiency, results and overall
economic development of the country. The labour movement has also tried to
show that it is actually the state that has been tampering with capitalism and
dressing it up as socialism. But that nobody should be fooled.

John Sichone noted that, "capitalists are already here in person or by proxy
and worse still we borrow their ugly money when our socialist banks run dry.
... Zambian annual budgets are more capitalist than one would be led to
believe". Further, he noted that international capitalist financial institutions
are already in Zambia, encouraged by the so-called socialist government of
Zambia: "The I.M.F. loan which bailed Zambia out of its economic strangula-
tion is more capitalist and we have to accept their capitalist conditions in order
to get it. Of late capitalists from the capitalist U.K. came to advise party and
its government on the running of its [socialist] parastatal organizations".[33] The
point being established here is that the government could not point a finger at
the labour movement as supportive of capitalism when in fact it was the
government that was much involved in capitalist exchanges. Chiluba was even
more blunt, "we have not created socialism and we have failed to dismiss
capitalism. We shall fight on".[34]

The labour movement has also demonstrated an acute awareness of class
inequalities in Zambia as well as the political consciousness to do something
about this state of affairs. At a public speech to trade unionists in 1980 for
example, Chiluba reported that "The incomes disparities in Zambia are such
that salaries of ten people in the high income bracket can account for the
incomes in wages of two hundred productive workers in the low income
bracket".[35] Further, in rejecting the K131 wage award given after the second
Turner Report the Labour leaders compared the class impact of the rising
inflation in the country, which to us demonstrates class consciousness. The
workers were awarded K156 instead which they also considered highly inad-

equate. To emphasize their point, they hypothesized about a man earning K150 per month, after noting that most workers in Zambia earn less than K100 a month. From this K150, the person had to pay: (1) P.A.Y.E. (pay as you earn), (2) Zambia National Provident Fund (Z.N.P.F.), (3) union dues. This person's earnings would drop to K130. From this K130, the person had to budget the following:[36]

Transport to and from work at 60 Ngwee daily	K14.00
House Rent	15.00
Charcoal and Firewood	20.00
Paraffin	5.00
Salt	1.20
Sugar	10.00
Bread	12.30
Water	10.00
Mealie Meal	13.86
Cooking Oil	9.00
Meat (once a month), relish, kapenta, beans, vegetables	40.00
Total	K160.76

From these figures ZCTU concluded in wonderment:

This worker is expected to live on the same commodities as the "apamwamba" (the rich) getting over a K1,000.00 a month plus free housing, free car, free "servants" etc. Whereas the children of the "apamwamba" are driven to school in company vehicles, the children of this poor worker have to struggle for a seat in crowded buses. When the labour movement in good faith tries to talk on behalf of this worker, they are called "reactionaries" and all other sorts of names. We know the facts are painful but please, let us do unto others as we would have them do unto us. After all, what is good for the dog must be good for the goat too.[37]

Political Involvement by the Working Class

To influence the situation for the betterment of workers in Zambia, the labour movement has expressed high level of interest and desire to be involved in political and socio-economic decision making. But not as incorporated workers or as appendages of the party and government. But as an autonomous party representing its constituency – the working class. This is the response of the labour leaders which expresses their view to the following Question: What kind of relationship would you like to see between the government and the workers? Timothy Walamba of the Mineworkers Union said:

> Workers do not enjoy confrontation with their government. But in order to avoid this, they would like their government to ensure that any major decision it makes, social, economic, and foreign should have the consideration of the effects. Such decisions would bear on workers. But as for today, most of the decisions made by the government seem to appease the outside world when workers in the country cannot even afford the very goods they produce. The Government today is not responsive to workers demands through mere discussions. It only becomes responsive after a nasty incident has occurred and then start witch-hunting the rubble-rouser.[38]

N. L. Simatendele of ZNUT said:

> I would like to see that suspicions have ended in approach to all national issues. A democratic dialogue be applied in approach to all national issues. Arm twisting by the employers be a thing of the past. The labour movement remains an independent organization with less control by the party and its government so that it will continue to speak freely and exercise democracy.[39]

Ignatius M. Kasumbu of the National Union of Commercial and Industrial Workers (NUCIW) also demanded more input by workers in national affairs:

1. The Government should open doors for worker's representatives who wish to meet them as regards workers' interests which is not the case unless there is so-called strike action.

2. We have already submitted changes in both Employment Act CAP No. 512 and Industrial Relations Act CAP. No. 517 of the Laws of Zambia but to our surprise nothing has been said from our friends in the government

3. At times we only receive directives to say negotiations between employers and National Union should be 10% which is against Labour Conventions No. 155 and 135 respectively.

4. There is a very strong rumour that labour movement will be turned into mass organization which we opposed two years back, what is their interests?[40]

J. Mubanga of the Railway Workers Union of Zambia (RWUZ) and L. B. Ikowa, National Chairman as well as S. I. Silwimba, National General Secretary of the National Union of Plantation and Agricultural Workers (N.U.P.A.W.) have demanded the autonomy of trade unions. To quote the latter two on the kind of relationship they envisage with the government:

The relationship that has no doubt of mind the guarantee of the labour movement membership to handle their problems without Government interference and without preconditions and restrictions of some kind to subjugate workers to some uncommon conditions like wage/salary increments, restrictions for long time when the present earnings do not meet the demands of the present marketed goods.[41]

Muvoywa M. Kaiko of the Zambia National Union of Teachers even expressed the desire for more fundamental political reforms:

Political power is very sweet. Politicians are interested in one-party state while unions want free political change. Full participation of the workers in freely electing their members of Parliament and the President.

1. Consideration on all political, social, and economic matters affecting the lives of the citizens and making decisions together.

2. Free and democratic system of elections based on the wishes of the people and not based on UNIP ticket.

3. The President of the party must be elected by the people in the provinces and not by a few individuals at Mulungushi Rock in Kabwe.

4. We would like to see the spirit of cooperation that was there between the labour movement and the Nationalists during the struggle for independence.

5. Finally we must share equitably the National *CAKE*. A very few people have eaten and are still eating three quarters of the National *CAKE*, why?[42]

The labour movement has also hailed the periodic election of labour leaders as Members of Parliament. They believe the election of more labour leaders as MP's will add extra power to the labour movement in the country. By 1979, there had been six labour leaders elected as Members of Parliament – Augustine Nkumbula the first General Secretary of ZCTU; Basil Kabwe, former ZCTU Secretary-General; Wilson Chakulya, former ZCTU Secretary-General; Saindani Phiri of MUZ; Chiwaya Pwalakasa, former MUZ branch official and Newstead Zimba, ZCTU Secretary General.[43] Whether the impact of these leaders once in parliament was progressive or not, the enthusiasm of the labour movement to their election shows intense desire to fully participate in national politics and hopefully to influence the situation for the betterment of workers in the process.

In 1991, Chiluba, ZCTU Chairman General became President of Zambia.

In the next chapter, I consider the broader implications on democracy for the working class struggles in Zambia.

Notes

1. Klaas Woldring, "Corruption and Inefficiency in Zambia - a survey of Recent Inquiries and Their Results" *Africa Today*, Vol.30, No.3, 1983, p. 74. For a contrary view of Zambian workers, especially MUZ, see *Africa Confidential*, Vol.27, No.9 (23 April, 1986).

2. For a discussion of the Instrument, see Ernest Beele, "The Bolting Workers: Some Scenarios of Statutory Instrument Number 6 of 1985" *Zambia Journal of Business*, Vol.4, No's. 1 and 2, 1985, pp. 27-29.

3. The Workers' Voice, Vol.2, No.18 (February 1985) p. 5.

4. Ibid., p. 2.

5. Ibid.

6. Ibid.

7. Ibid.

8. Beele, note 2.

9. Ibid., p. 27.

10. "Symposium Resolves" *The Workers Voice*, Vol.3, No. 2 (September 1980) p. 7.

11. Beele, note 2, p. 28.

12. Muvoywa M. Kaiko, ZNUT (16th March, 1987).

13. M. K. Sumani, MUZ, written statement to author, no date but in early 1987.

14. Kaiko, note 12.

15. Timothy Walamba, MUZ (11th March, 1987).

16. Sumani, note 13.

17. Jeff Crisp, *The Story of an African Working Class* (London: Zed Press, 1984).

18. Ibid., p. 183.

19. Ibid., p. 185. For a study of Ghanaian railwaymen, see Richard Jeffries, *Class, Power and Ideology in Ghana: The Railwaymen of Sekondi* (London: Cambridge University Press, 1978).

20. Crisp, note 17, p. 185.

21. Ibid., p. 187.

22. Ibid.

23. Walamba, note 15.

24. *The Workers' Voice*, note 10, p. 7.

25. Ibid.

26. Walamba, note 15.

27. *The Workers Voice*, Vol.3, No.1 (June 1980) p. 4.

28. *The Workers Voice*, Vol.3, No.3 (October 1980) p. 8.

29. Ibid.

30. Ibid.

31. *The Workers Voice*, note 10, p. 7.

32. See Patu Simoko, *Sunday Times of Zambia* (27 July, 1980).

33. Sichone, note 28, p. 8.

34. Chiluba, *The Workers Voice*, note 10, p. 2.

35. Ibid.

36. "Cost of Living Too High: Painful Facts" *The Workers Voice*, note 27, p. 3.

37. Ibid.

38. Note 15.

39. N. L. Simatendele, Zambia National Union of Teachers (16 March, 1987).

40. Ignatius M. Kasumbu, National Union of Commercial and Industrial Workers (16 March, 1987).

41. L. B. Ikowa and S. I. Silwimba, National Union of Plantation and Agricultural Workers (16 March, 1987).

42. Muvoywa, note 12. Multi-Party Politics were introduced in 1990.

43. See *The Workers Voice*, Vol.2, No.5 (January 1979) p. 4.

9

Labour Unions and the State in Zambia:
A Conclusion up to 1989

The Zambian Labour movement is neither revolutionary in the sense of wanting to overthrow the existing regime by revolutionary means and usher in a new era, nor is it a reactionary force intent on supporting the preservation of existing backward conditions. Instead this study has shown that the Zambian labour movement is interested in and supports political and economic processes in Zambia that are responsive firstly to the interests of the working class and secondly to the mass of the people in Zambia. Because of the nature of the state – one-party (up to 1990) and largely pro-capitalist state despite its socialist claims, any interventionist politics by the labour movement would face this structural constraint. But the labour movement has refrained from any serious interventionist politics – preferring instead to be autonomous from politics while issuing critical commentaries on the State's political and economic programmes. The labour movement has been more reactive than proactive. Its reactive stance can be categorised as being within the mould of social democracy – pluralist democracy free from authoritarianism. Social democracy is what the Zambian labour movement seems to be fighting for.

Can the Zambian labour movement do more than merely issue critiques and react to state policies? Can it go beyond social democracy? The answer seems to be in the affirmative. One of the strongest achievements of the ZCTU is its educational activities within the labour movement. I think this programme of education can be extended more vigorously to the rest of the population. A lot has already been done in this area but more could be done to make the general population more aware of the alternative visions of the labour movement. Of course the extent to which this educational activity can be carried to has to be assessed so that the party-state does not clamp heavily to stem this activity. It may be that the educational programme of ZCTU is limited because of the limited vision of the labour movement itself. As already stated, the labour movement in Zambia has no revolutionary programme, its concerns are more social democratic in nature. Even genuine democracy cannot be achieved as long as a one-party state exists.

It is also possible that the state has not totally desired much as it has attempted, to take over the labour movement like in Tanzania and other African countries because the threat posed by the labour movement has not been so serious. It may be that the state is genuinely interested in a semi-autonomous labour movement in order to preserve industrial peace in the country. The state has perhaps recognized that whether or not the labour movement is under state control, there may always be serious strikes. It may also be that the strong roots of the labour movement dating back to the colonial days was a disincentive to the State to try to totally take it over. I am inclined to the conclusion that all the above suggestions partially explain the outcome of the state – labour stalemate in Zambia. The labour movement on the other hand seems to know its limits.

My main interest in the Zambian labour movement as chronicled in this study is that it has contributed to the development of a democratic space in Zambia. This has been due to its struggle for autonomy from the state. It is the only social force that has survived the onslaught of the state. All other would-be contenders to State monopoly eg. opposition politicians; students; intellectuals; the media, etc. have been crushed. The easiness with which these possible opposition centres were crushed testifies to their weakness in the first place. And this goes back to the nature of the social forces produced by colonialism. Colonialism produced a very strong labour movement which still survives. However, hardly any intellectuals centred in the arts were produced. The media base was weak. Hardly any politicians of independent means of existence to challenge the party-state existed either at independence or in 1973 when the one-party state came into existence. There are still no intellectuals to speak of in Zambia, most of those who could exist have sought careers within the ever-expanding party machinery. The media is controlled by the state. The independent bourgeoisie most of whom acquired their wealth while they were still employed by the state are comfortably enjoying their fortunes. Politics is not in their minds. The message here is that strong and autonomous entities are prerequisites to democracy. Where they are weak or are not autonomous, democracy may be tenuous.

However if the limited programme of the Zambian labour movement is to be realized, the support and alliance of students, intellectuals and the media are indispensable. But these sectors have no programme of support or alliance either. The reasons for this are already given above; they have been crushed or incorporated in the party-state structures. It is not surprising that the Zambian labour movement is going it alone. And that is why despite its limited programme, the labour movement can count on my support in their struggle for democracy.

Most of what has been written in this chapter has been overtaken by events since early 1990. The following chapters update the situation. I have left his chapter intact as this was my thinking up to 1989.

Postscript
March 1991

10

The Crisis of the One-Party State System in Zambia

E vents in Eastern Europe where peoples' demands for social, political and economic transformation led to the political collapse and reconstitution of many states, reverberated in Africa.[1] In Zambia, as described elsewhere there were already some businessmen who had clamoured since the early 1980s for multi-party politics. Trade unions in Zambia had been campaigning for political and economic accountability for a very long time. The crisis in Eastern Europe gave them new impetus and they started to organize openly. Because of internal and external pressure, the political leadership promised a referendum on this issue to be held in October 1990, but then postponed it to August 1991. President Kaunda later said he would change the constitution rather than call for a referendum. Multi-party politics were permitted in 1990 by an amendment to article 4 of the Constitution of Zambia which had forbidden the formation of political parties other than UNIP.

The struggle for multi-party politics was circumscribed by severe economic crisis in the country. In the process of implementing the International Monetary Fund (IMF) austerity measures, to stem the economic crisis in Zambia, the government substantially increased the price of mealie meal in June 1990. On June 25, 1990, University of Zambia students in Lusaka rioted against the price increases.

They were joined by ordinary people in Lusaka. In the process of quelling the riots, the police shot to death more than 30 people. The riots spread to other towns. Once again, fulfilling IMF conditions, as in 1986, had brought about rioting by ordinary people. Once again the government used repressive tactics. Once again the government blamed the "enemies" of the government as the perpetrators of "disorder". In the midst of this crisis over mealie meal, a section of the army announced over the radio on June 30, 1990 that they had overthrown the government. There was much jubilation in Lusaka and elsewhere. The coup attempt, however, was very shortlived, it lasted only about 5 hours. It however, underscored most dramatically, unlike anything before, the unpopularity of the Zambian political regime.

The attempted military coup further fuelled the advocates for a multi-party system. The Zambian trade union movement has been part of the coalition advocating for the transformation of the political system from one-party state to multi-party state. In December 1990, the Parliament of Zambia approved the Bill to turn Zambia into a multi-party system and shortly afterwards, President Kaunda signed the Bill into law. It is however very important to review the history of the one-party system so that justifications for it should never be made again. It is important to learn from history.

The One-Party State in Zambia

When Zambia became independent in 1964, it was a multi-party system – there was the United National Independence Party (UNIP) and the African National Congress (ANC), the former being the ruling party. For many years the leadership of the ruling party expressed the view that a one-party system in Zambia will only come through the ballot box and not through imposition. For example addressing the annual general conference of UNIP at Mulungushi on 15th August 1967, President Kaunda declared:

> If what has been happening at both the Parliamentary and Local Government levels is anything to go by, we are obviously very close to the attainment of the one-party state.

And further:

> ... being honest to the cause of the common man we would, through effective Party and Government organizations, paralyse and wipe out any opposition thereby bringing about the birth of a one-party state... We go further and declare that even when this comes about we would not (sic!) legislate against the formation of opposition parties because we might be bottling the feelings of certain people no matter how few... I repeat, one-party state is coming to Zambia because the masses of our people recognize that we are sincere and true to each one of them... The masses of our people trust us because we have said that the one-party state was

going to come about as a result of the people voting for the party freely for a people's democracy and this has continued to be our guideline.[2]

These optimistic views were expressed as a result of massive electoral successes UNIP had been registering in local elections between 1964 and 1967. But the picture was to dramatically change in 1967. This was the year (1967) when the first post-independence elections for the members of the Central Committee were held. Posts in this Committee were crucial and those who held them wielded tremendous power and influence over the decision-making process which allocated scarce resources to regions, communities and individuals in Zambia. Thus, stiff competition arose in UNIP over the posts in the Central Committee. Within UNIP however, the political groups that competed for the control of the party's/government policies were generally ethnic or regional groups.[3] These groups had to respond to their constituents in the provinces, regions and localities. This party factionalism and sectionalism within UNIP was first evident in 1966 when the United Party (UP) was formed by dissidents from UNIP. The UP was the product of the growing disenchantment and relative deprivation felt by many political leaders of Lozi origin within UNIP over what they regarded as the neglect of Barotseland (now Western Province) in terms of system distributive outputs and also in view of what they regarded as Bemba dominance of the party.[4] UP however, did not pose any serious threat to UNIP until after the crisis in UNIP in 1967.

The 1967 elections saw the decline in power of politicians from eastern (Ngoni) and western (Lozi) provinces. They were edged out by the coalition of politicians from northern (Bemba) and southern (Tonga) provinces. Thus the stage for bitter intra-party factional fighting had started. President Kaunda presented the gloomy picture in the party when he stated during the elections:

> We have canvassed so strongly and indeed, viciously, along tribal, racial and provincial lines, that one wonders whether we really have national or tribal and provincial leadership. I must admit publicly that I have never experienced in the life of this young nation, such a spate of hate, based entirely on tribe, province, race, colour and religion, which is the negation of all that we stand for in this Party and Government. I do not think that we can blame the common man for this. The fault is ours fellow leaders – we, the people here assembled.[5]

In the 1968 elections, the ANC gained some seats due to the swelling up of its ranks by the members of the UP which was banned just before the elections. This was an immediate indication that the ANC was not going to suffer a natural death as had been hoped. Meanwhile, in UNIP, factional competition that had been unleashed by the 1967 elections continued festering. In 1969, those politicians who had been edged out in 1967, began to form coalitions to fight the next round of elections which were to be held in 1970. Sensing the tension and possible electoral disaster, the vice-president, Simon Kapwepwe resigned his post in 1970 and eventually from the party and government in August 1971. Shortly thereafter he formed the United Progressive Party (UPP), the most formidable opposition party to Kaunda's UNIP to date. Kapwepwe whose constituency was based on the copperbelt and in northern province quickly gathered support from some key members from UNIP, the Copperbelt, Northern Province and elsewhere. Members of the disgruntled petty bourgeoisie were also defecting from UNIP. There was a likely coalition with the ANC. And the election was just round the corner in 1972. It was clear UNIP was in a crisis and something had to be done or it would go down in defeat.

The Party-State reacted quickly and harshly to the threat of the possible loss of power. The new opposition and its leader Simon Kapwepwe were rounded up and detained under the pretext of threat to public security: Emergency powers were invoked to detain the opposition members. The evolution of the law of detention in Zambia will be dealt with shortly.

It was in this political context that the one-party system became inevitable and it was to be dressed in appropriate garb. On 25th February 1972, President Kaunda put forward his *raison d' etre* for opting for a one-party state:

You know that since Independence there has been a constant demand for the establishment of a one-party state in Zambia. The demands have increasingly become more and more widespread in all corners of Zambia. In recent months I have received hundreds of messages and letters from organizations and individuals appealing to me to take concrete steps to bring about a One-Party system of Government. In the resolutions passed by almost every conference, whether political or non-political, unequivocal demands have been made for Government to introduce a One-Party system of Government. Chiefs last year joined the chorus of the overwhelming majority of the people. Indeed, the UNIP National Council sitting in Mulungushi Hall between the 1st and the 3rd October last year charged the Central Committee of the ruling party to work towards the achievement of a One-Party Democracy in which the liberties and welfare of the common man will be paramount. The Central Committee in its study of the subject noted that in this overwhelming public demand the objective for calling for a new system of Government is the fundamental need to preserve unity, strengthen peace and accelerate development in freedom and justice.[6]

He went further to state that "The Government had decided that Zambia shall become a one-party participatory Democracy and that practical steps should be taken to implement the decision".[7] Thus it was not the people but the government who decided to form a one-party state system. The first practical step was the appointment of a "National Commission to consider and recommend changes in the Constitution of the Republic of Zambia, the constitution of UNIP and matters related thereto necessary to bring about the establishment of a one-party participatory Democracy in Zambia."[8] The National Commission was headed by Mainza Chona, the vice-president who had replaced Simon Kapwepwe when the latter resigned. The report[9] of the National Commission diverged quite markedly in some respects from the intentions of the party and government as the government's own white paper[10] showed. The purpose of having had a National Commission seemed absurd. Let us follow some areas of the report and the government's response closely – the areas of Preamble, Human Rights, the Executive, Parliament and Elections.[11]

The Preamble:

The commission discussed the need for a Preamble to the proposed Constitution of a One-Party Participatory Democracy which would, among other things, reflect the "sentiments and aspirations of the people of Zambia". In this regard there was an important innovative creation in the Preamble, in that while the Constitution of Zambia's First Republic clearly lacked a political profile, the recommendations of the Commission made it imperative that the people of Zambia legitimize the dramatic institutional changes in the state power structure following the decision to introduce a one-party system and that this popular legitimation be codified in the Preamble to the new Constitution.

The government's White Paper accepted the Commission's recommendations but moved a step further to incorporate in the first paragraph of the Preamble the ideological superstructure of the regime: the Philosophy of Humanism.

Historically speaking, the use of ideology as an instrument of political rule and the strategy for social and economic changes in Zambia, had been an important feature of President Kaunda's approach towards development.[12] This notwithstanding, its application had hitherto remained outside the confines of the constitutional structure. However, by specifically incorporating it in the Preamble the aim here was to legalize President Kaunda's thoughts and prescriptions for Zambia and to institutionalize Humanism as the official ideology of the new system and a guiding compass of all the people as a whole.[13] As already seen, this study does not dwell very much on the role of the ideology of humanism in class struggles in Zambia.

Human Rights:

After due consideration of the issue of the protection of the fundamental rights and freedoms of the individual under various subheadings the Commission made a number of recommendations. With regard to the issue of personal liberty, restrictions and detentions, the Commission recommended:

1. That there should be no detention without trial except during the period of emergency.

2. That a detainee or restrictee should be furnished with a written statement within a period of ten days specifying the reasons for his detention or restriction.

3. That the notification of detention or restriction should be published in the Government Gazette within fourteen days of such detention or restriction.

4. That a tribunal be established within three months to review the detention or restriction and that its decision should be binding on the authority.

5. That the composition of the tribunal should consist of three persons – the Chairman and two other persons one of whom should be a lawyer – and that the appointment of the tribunal should be made by the Chief Justice in consultation with the President.

6. That the detainees be free to communicate with both their relatives and their lawyers and that they should not be held incommunicado.

7. That whenever a state of emergency is declared while the Parliament is not in session or after its dissolution that it should be summoned within twenty-eight days from the date of the proclamation of such emergency.

8. That a declaration of the state of emergency should cease after six months from the date of the proclamation unless the National Assembly approves its continuation.

The government accepted the recommendation of the Commission for the retention of the provisions within the Constitution under which detentions and restrictions could be effected, but rejected all of the other safeguards suggested by the Commission which were intended to obviate any abuse of power by the executive. The reason for the rejection being that:

... the Government felt that at this stage in the nation's development and in view of Zambia's geo-political position in Southern Africa these recommendations could not be implemented without detriment to Zambia's security and sovereignty.[14]

Emergency regulations have been invoked in order to detain so many people, including labour leaders as we have already seen and shall see later.

The Executive:

The Commission examined the issue of the executive against the background of the nature of politics under the multi-party system and recommended (1) "that there be a President with specified executive powers supported by a Prime Minister who would be responsible for Government administration", and (2) that the functions of the President should include among other things:

1. Serving as the Head of State and President of the Party.

2. Assuming supreme responsibility in matters of defence and national security.

3. The appointment of a Prime Minister from among Members of Parliament subject to the approval of the National Assembly.

4. The appointment of such public officers as he is specifically empowered under the Republican and Party Constitutions.

5. The appointment of the Secretary-General of the Party from among members of the Central Committee subject to the approval of the National Council.

The government accepted the idea of the separation of functions of the President from that of the Prime Minister but amended the recommendations with respect to the scope of presidential powers by giving the President full executive powers both in Republican and Party Constitutions. The government justified this amendment on the grounds that:

Zambia has many enemies surrounding her and therefore the implementation of the One-Party Participatory Democracy as well as Humanism, together with the attendant problems, require a unified command under an Executive President.[15]

The government had different views with respect to certain aspects of the election of the President. For instance the Commission recommended that the

President be popularly elected and that the nomination period be thirty days. In addition it also recommended that if there should be only one candidate after the expiry of the nomination period that "the candidate be presented to the electorate for confirmation by a simple majority". However, while the government accepted the idea of popular election, it reduced the nomination period to ten days. Above all, it rejected the Commission's suggestion that the sole candidate after the nomination period be presented to the electorate for confirmation. Rather it decided that "if after the nomination period there is only one candidate, he shall be deemed elected".[16]

With regard to the tenure of office, the Commission recommended that the President's term of office be five years and that he be eligible for a second term of five years after which he should not be eligible for a period of at least five years. After this period he could stand for a new term of five years. The Government rejected this suggestion and decided instead "that there should be no limitation on how often a man or woman can serve his or her country in the Office of President".[17] Thus in effect sanctioning a life presidency under a one-party state system.

Cabinet:

The Commission recommended that the Prime Minister should be appointed by the President amongst Members of Parliament subject to the approval of the Parliament and that he should be responsible for the execution of the following functions:

1.   To serve as the Head of Cabinet and to preside over Cabinet meetings.

2.   To serve as the chief spokesman on government matters.

3.   To appoint Ministers and Deputy Ministers in consultation with the President; and to appoint the Attorney-General of the Republic from amongst the Members of Parliament in consultation with the President.

The Commission also recommended that the Prime Minister shall retain his office at the pleasure of the President and/or Parliament.

The government rejected these recommendations arguing that in view of its decision that the full executive powers of the Republic be vested in the President, accordingly that the Prime Minister be appointed by and should continue to retain his office at the pleasure of the President. Besides, the government decided that the functions of the Prime Minister should be restricted to serving as the head of government administration as well as the leader of government business in Parliament. And that in the absence of the Prime Minister the President should appoint a Minister to act. It was also decided that the Secretary-General of the Party should be an ex-officio member of Cabinet.

Parliament:

The Commission's recommendations on the nature of Parliament suitable to Zambia's one-party system as well as its composition did not meet strong opposition from the government, except in two areas namely: *(a)* the size of members to be nominated, *(b)* institutional representation in Parliament. The Commission had envisaged a Parliament of 136 members of which 115 should be elected, 17 to be drawn from the elected members of religious, educational, civil service, trade union organizations, Youth Council, Commerce and Industry, the security forces and the National Women's Council, while three were to be nominated by the President, plus the Speaker of the National Assembly. The government agreed with the Commission regarding the total number of members but rejected the idea of institutional representation. Institutional representation could, I believe, have democratized politics to some extent. Further, instead of three the government decided that the President should nominate ten persons to Parliament.

Equally, the government made only a slight modification with regard to the required qualifications for election to the National Assembly. In fact it agreed to almost all that the Commission had to say in this regard except with respect to age, which the government placed at 21 years instead of 18 as suggested by the Commission. It later turned out that people who wanted to stand for parliamentary elections had to be approved by the central committee. The aim may have been to create a "dummy parliament".

Elections:

A more contentious issue was with regard to the conduct of elections to the National Assembly. The Commission recommended that:

1. All qualified Zambian citizens should be free to stand for parliamentary elections.

2. It was not necessary to have primary elections in the One-Party Participatory Democracy.

3. The Party should undertake the necessary organizational arrangements to introduce prospective candidates to the electorate and that

thereafter the candidates should be free to organize and conduct their own individual campaigns at their own expense.

4. The Prime Minister and his Cabinet should resign during the period of parliamentary elections and that within this period all executive powers should be vested in the President who should feel free to recall the outgoing Cabinet in the case of a national crisis.

The government accepted only the first recommendation. It not only decided that there should be primary elections, but also as already said, in order to underscore the supremacy of the Party, the government decided that the names of all candidates intending to contest parliamentary elections once elected by the regional conference of the Party must be submitted to the Central Committee for vetting. The whole Central Committee was appointed by the President. The government agreed, however, to organize public meetings to introduce prospective parliamentary candidates. Contrary to the suggestion of the Commission, the government made it clear that all electoral campaigns would "be financed and conducted by, and under the supervision of, the Party".[18]

Using the government White Paper, the government proclaimed Zambia a presidential one-party system on 13th December, 1972. The 1964 constitution was replaced in 1973 by a new constitution which declared "a one-party participatory democracy under the philosophy of Humanism". Article 4 states:

1. There shall be one and only one political party organization in Zambia, namely, the United National Independence Party ...

2. Nothing contained in this Constitution shall be so construed as to entitle any person lawfully to form or attempt to form any political party or organization other than the Party, or to belong to, assemble or associate with or express opinion or do any other thing in sympathy with, such political party or organization.

The beneficiary of the new system was obviously the president who was given wide powers as well as the bureaucratic bourgeoisie. Theoretically, the highest organ of the party at the national level is the General Conference which meets every five years. The General Conference elects the President of the Party and 20 members of the Central Committee.

Delegates to the General Conference must be members of the party drawn from the following sources:

1. All members of the National Council.

2.   About 600 delegates from each province selected in accordance with the general procedures laid down by the Central Committee.

3.   One delegate representing each of the trade unions affiliated to the Zambia Congress of Trade Unions.

4.   One delegate from each of the organizations affiliated to the Party.

Next in line in national importance is the National Council which meets twice a year. The National Council is the policy-making body of the Party. It is empowered to discuss, adopt and review decisions made by the Central Committee as well as to pass any resolutions or to make recommendations for specific proposals of legislative, financial or administrative nature to be included in the party programme.[19]

The National Council consisted of the following people:

1.   Members of the Central Committee.

2.   Members of Parliament.

3.   Provincial Political Secretaries.

4.   District Governors.

5.   Three officials, including the Regional Secretary, from each region.

6.   Ten representatives of the security forces.

7.   Six representatives elected by the Zambia Congress of Trade Unions.

8.   One representative from each organization affiliated to the Party.

9.   Heads of Zambian missions abroad.

10.   The administrative and the Executive Officers at the Party's National Headquarters.

11.   Members of the Executive Committee of the Women's Brigade.

12.   Members of the Executive Committee of the Youth Brigade.

Apart from invited guests (usually heads of foreign missions in Zambia), the managing directors of parastatal bodies, the Vice-Chancellor of the University of Zambia and other public officials closely affiliated to or directly under the control of the Party/government including permanent secretaries normally attended the opening session of the National Council in which President Kaunda traditionally delivered major policy addresses that form the basis of the deliberations and resolutions of the National Council.[20] The delegates attending the General Conference and National Council were defined as "Leaders" – any person holding a specified office within the party/government and parastatal bodies as well as the ZCTU etc.

Thus the principles of "Participatory Democracy" were supposed to be enshrined in the above party state and governmental arrangements. Note that representatives from worker's unions were also directly represented at the General Conference and National Council. Unions like all other organizations were supposed to be integrated in the party and not appear to be operating from outside the party structures. The labour leaders stated, however, that their participation in the party (UNIP) should not be seen as incorporation or loss of autonomy. Zimba, ZCTU's Secretary General articulated the labour movement's stand on the question:

> There should be a clear distinction in interpreting the Z.C.T.U. and its Affiliates' existence in the Party's Constitution. This is meant for us to participate in political gatherings and decision-making assemblies. This does not mean fusion of the two organizations. The question of affiliation to the Party was enshrined in the old constitution which was amended.

> We continue to operate as a Labour Movement representative of the workers. Some leadership in political circles still think we are affiliated to the Party as we hear them say.[21]

A central question which is relevant to this chapter is whether the institution of the one-party state affected the human rights record in Zambia. This is relevant in the sense that the ruling party may have been constrained in dealing decisively with the people between 1964 and 1972 for fear of driving the electorate to the opposition.[22] Did the banning of the opposition enable the ruling party state to deal with the people more decisively? I have suggested that the state tried but failed to tame the working class.

The Law of Detention[23]

We have already seen that this is another crucial state repressive instrument. Its history is worth recounting briefly. Its implications for class struggles have already been shown.

Detention had been a common feature in colonial Zambia and by Ordinance No. 5 of 1960, the Legislative Council of Northern Rhodesia enacted the Preservation of Public Security Ordinance, s.4 of which reads as follows:

"4. (1) If at any time the Governor is satisfied that the situation in the Territory is so grave that the exercise of the powers conferred by section three of the Ordinance is inadequate to ensure the preservation of public security, he may by Proclamation declare that the provisions of sub-section (2) of this section shall come into operation accordingly; and they shall continue in operation until the Governor by a further Proclamation directs that they shall cease to have effect except as respects things previously done or omitted to be done.

(2) The Governor may, for the preservation of public security, make regulations to provide, so far as appears to him to be strictly required by the exigencies of the situation in the Territory, for –

(a) the detention of persons;

(b) requiring persons to do work and render services."

On July 28th, 1964, the Governor, by Government Notice No. 376, issued Proclamation No. 5 under which he declared and proclaimed the coming into force on that date of the provisions of s.4(2) of the Preservation of Public Security Ordinance. On the same date the Governor, by Government Notice No. 377, amended the Preservation of Public Security Regulations by the introduction, among other things, of Regulation 31A in these terms:

"31A (1) Whenever the Governor is satisfied that for the purpose of preserving public security it is necessary to exercise control over any person, directing that such person be detained and thereupon such person shall be arrested and detained."

It is a notorious fact that the immediate purpose of the measures taken then was to deal with the disturbances brought about in parts of the Northern and the Eastern Provinces by members of the Lumpa Church.[24]

When Northern Rhodesia became the Republic of Zambia on October 24th, 1964, s.2(1) of the Zambia Independence Act of that year provided:

"2. (1) Subject to the following provisions of this Act, on and after the appointed day (i.e. October 24th, 1964) all law or a provision of an Act of Parliament or of any other enactment or instrument whatsoever, is in force on that day or has been passed or made before that day and comes into force thereafter, shall, unless and until provision to the contrary is made by Parliament or some other authority having power in that behalf, have the same operation in relation to Zambia, and persons and things belonging to or connected with Zambia, as it would have apart from this subsection if on the appointed day Northern Rhodesia had been renamed Zambia but there had been no change in its status."

It was stipulated further,

"4. (1) Subject to the provisions of this section, the existing laws shall, notwithstanding the revocation of the existing Orders or the establishment of a Republic in Zambia, continue in force after the commencement of this Order as if they had been made in pursuance of this Order.

(6) For the purposes of this section, the existing laws' means all Ordinances, laws or statutory instruments having effect as part of the law of Northern Rhodesia ..."

Thus the emergency declaration of July 28th, 1964 continued after independence. It was for a duration of six months and by a resolution passed on April 21st, 1965, the National Assembly extended the life of the declaration for a further period of six months.[25]

This extension was followed by six-monthly renewals of the declaration until s.8 of the *Constitution (Amendment) (No. 5) Act, 1969*, made the six-monthly renewals unnecessary. As a result of the amendment, the declaration continues in force for an indefinite period unless and until it is revoked by either the President or the National Assembly. As there has been no revocation, the declaration is to date still in force under the provisions of s.15 of the *Constitution of Zambia Act, 1973*. As we saw above when discussing the one-party state system, democratic reforms to emergency powers were denied by the Government.

Thus while the State was organizing the Zambians under the one-party system, an undercurrent of state repressive apparatus was also being enshrined permanently. The institution of the one-party system was a trend towards authoritarianism and so was the institutionalization of permanent emergency powers.

Multi-Party Politics

It is fitting that the struggle towards a multi-party system in Zambia incorporated the demand for the repeal of the emergency laws. There must also be a demand to put the army into its proper place in a democracy.

For over fifteen years after the institutionalisation of the one-party state system, it was taboo to talk about multi-partyism in Zambia. Article 4 of the Constitution of Zambia as already pointed out forbade the formation of other political parties. Even if the Chona Commission had made a recommendation that the country's constitutional arrangements be reviewed every ten years, this never happened.[26]

In an address to the National Council of UNIP in May 1990, President Kaunda strongly recommended that the call for multi-partyism be rejected. But the riots and attempted military coup of June and July 1990 forced his hand and accepted the principle of multi-partyism. The Umbrella Movement for Multi-party Democracy (MMD) constituted itself as a advocacy group for multi-partyism. When President Kaunda signed into law the Bill to permit the existence of other parties in December 1990, the MMD reconstituted itself into a political party.

The MMD is the biggest of the new parties and so far contained well-known political and trade union personalities: Chiluba of ZCTU; Robinson Nabulyato, former speaker of the National Assembly; Arthur Wina, former Finance Minister; Vernon Mwaanga, former Foreign Minister and Central Committee Member; Andrew Kashita, former Mines Minister; Levy Mwanawasa, former Solicitor-General; Humphrey Mulemba, former Secretary-General; Ludwig Sondashi, former Central Committee Member and others.[27] This was an impressive collection of individuals who had at one time or another served UNIP very well.

That the ruling party took MMD seriously and that it was threatened politically can be gleaned from some of the actions or statements levelled against the MMD.

President Kaunda repeatedly accused MMD advocates of inciting the army and mineworkers to disrupt the country in order to weaken the power of UNIP. He also accused them of soliciting military support from a rebel leader in neighbouring Angola.[28] Kaunda also directed the *Zambia Daily Mail*, the *Times of Zambia* and the Zambia National Broadcasting Corporation not to cover MMD activities but this was overturned by the High Court in Lusaka.[29] The Secretary-General of UNIP, Grey Zulu even went to court to apply against the use of some political symbols by the MMD. Kaunda also refused to repeal the repressive emergency powers on the pretext that MMD behaviour militates against this. Scanning Zambian newspapers disclosed morbid fear of the MMD by UNIP.

MMD policies included free enterprise, limited state intervention in the economy, genuine concern for the poor, improving dilapidated eduction, health and other services and facilities. UNIP is seen to have messed all these up over the years and in the context of the ever declining economy, UNIP had cause to feel threatened.[30]

Sichone maintains that the bringing-in of a one-party state system in Zambia was a sign of weakness on the part of UNIP, just as the one-party state is an admission of weakness rather than strength on the part of the post-colonial state in general.[31] I will extend this argument to suggest that the ushering in of multi-partyism in Zambia was also a sign of weakness on the party of UNIP. It could no longer sustain the dominance it had acquired under the one-party state system and at the same time it could no longer prevent other competing interests from participating in political life. The coercive instruments of the state ie emergency powers which have been used to detain individuals have been rendered inoperative by the forces of change. These repressive instruments could be used anytime, however, since they had not been repealed, alternatively other subtle forms of repression may be found or resuscitated. One such form of subtle repression was the existence and operations of UNIP militants who had gone around harassing and intimidating opposition members and the party state had turned a blind eye.[32]

The existence of these UNIP militants and their unchallenged power-play made it more urgent to secure more firmly the culture of multi-party politics in Zambia. This will be a continuing challenge. The UNIP leadership will also have to mature politically and stop attributing bad motives on the part of their opponents. Everything will ultimately depend on the balance of power between the various social groups and their relationship to the state and economy.

Notes

1. See also Geoff Zulu, "Multiparty Politics: Where to" *Zambia Daily Mail* Dec. 3, 1990, p. 4.

2. Zambia Information Services, *Mulungushi Conference - proceedings of the Annual General Conference of the United National Independence Party held at Mulungushi 14-20th August 1967* Lusaka: Government Printer, pp. 10-11.

3. Patrick Ollawa, *Participatory Democracy in Zambia: The Political Economy of National Development*, IlFracombe: Arthur H. Stockwell Ltd., 1979) p. 238.

4. Ibid., p. 240.

5. Zambia Information Services, note 2, p. 52.

6. Republic of Zambia, *Report of the National Commission on the Establishment of a One-Party Participatory Democracy in Zambia* (Chona Commission), (Lusaka: Government Printer, 1972).

7. Ibid., p. 1.

8. Ibid., i.

9. Republic of Zambia, *Reports of the Working Party Appointed to Review the System of Decentralised Administration.* Lusaka: Cabinet Office, 1972 Appendix I, p. 67.

10. Republic of Zambia, *Report of the National Commission on the Establishment of a One-Party Participatory Democracy in Zambia: Summary of Recommendations Accepted by Government* (Government Paper No. 1 of 1972) (Lusaka: Government Printer, 1972).

11. See notes 9 and 10. See also summary in Ollawa, note 3. I am indebted to Ollawa for analysis in the following sections. For a comprehensive study of the Zambian one party state system, see Morris Szeftel et al. *The Dynamics of the one party state in Zambia* (Manchester: Manchester University Press, 1984).

12. Kenneth Kaunda, *Humanism in Zambia and A Guide to its Implementation*, (Lusaka: State House, 1974).

13. Ollawa, note 3, p. 255.

14. Republic of Zambia, note 10, p. 3.

15. Ibid., p. 4.

16. Ibid.

17. Ibid., p. 5.

18. Ibid., p. 11.

19. Ollawa, note 3, p. 279.

20. Ibid.

21. The Workers Voice, Vol. 3, No. 1 (June, 1980) p. 7.

22. The point raised by Anirudha Gupta, "Trade Unionism and Politics on the Copperbelt" in *Politics in Zambia* edited by William Tordoff (Manchester: Manchester University Press, 1974) pp. 288-320.

23. This section relies on the ruling in *Shamwana Versus Attorney-General* (Supreme Court, 1980) reprinted in *Civil Liberties Cases in Zambia* by Muna Ndulo and Kaye Tuner, Oxford: 1984, pp. 175-182. See also Paulsen Himwiinga, *Emergency Powers in Zambia*, LLM Dissertation, University of Zambia, 1984.

24. Shamwana Versus Attorney-General, note 23, p. 177.

25. National Assembly Debates, Vol. III (April-May, 1965) p. 9.

26. See Geoff Zulu, note 1.

27. See *Africa Confidential* vol. 31, no. 20, 12 October 1990, pp. 6-7.

28. See among numerous reports, *Sunday Times of Zambia* December 2, 1990, p.1.

29. Times of Zambia February 19, 1991, p. 1.

30. See on MMD's policies, *Zambia Daily Mail*, February 23, 1991, p.1.

31. Owen B. Sichone, "One-Party Participatory Democracy and Socialist Orientation: The De-Politicization of the Masses in Post-Colonial Zambia" in Peter Meyns and Dani Wadada Nabudere (eds.) *Democracy and the One-Party-State in Africa* (Hamburg: Institut Fr Afrika-Kunde, 1989), pp.131-2 and *passim*.

32. See Sichone, Ibid.

11

Political Democracy, Economic Crises and the Challenges Ahead

Multi-party politics are a giant step in the transformation of Zambia's political system. This political transformation will be threatened constantly by economic crises besetting the country, not to mention the ever watchful army. It is important to review in this chapter Zambia's economic crises by way of conclusion.

Zambia is in deep economic crises. It has been so for a very long time. In 1990 the debt stood at US$7.2 billion. Zambia could not afford to pay the interest, not to talk about the principal of this debt. To survive, Zambia has depended on more borrowing and asking for reschedulings of its debt.

Zambia has tried many strategies to overcome its predicament, all of them seem to have been forced on the government. The government seems to have had no initiatives of its own.[1]

Zambia has tried the remedy of individual disengagement from the IMF.[2] In December 1986 people rioted in Zambia's cooperbelt towns – the copper producing and heaviest urbanized region of Zambia – against government imposed IMF austerity measures. The IMF had wanted the imposition of 120 percent increase in the price of maize meal, Zambia's staple food. In May 1987, President Kaunda, announced that Zambia would restrict its debt repayments to 10 percent of its net export earnings.[3] At that time interest payment on loans was taking up 30 percent of the country's export earnings.[4] He also severed all ties to the IMF. The president stated that since 1973 the government's efforts to implement the diffusionist policies of the IMF had led to a fall in living standards and rising unemployment. He directed the IMF to consider this: "...which is a better partner – a nation which devotes all of its resources to paying debts and therefore grinds to an economic and political halt, or a stable nation, capable of sustaining the repayment of its entire debt?"[5] The IMF while scared of its image as a result of Zambia's actions, could not care less so long they maintained the "ties that bind" with Zambia or any other developing country.

The "ties that bind" between Zambia and the IMF (and typical of many other countries) started in the following manner. At independence in 1964, Zambia a copper rich country inherited black Africa's largest industrial base. It had a positive balance of payments account. Unfortunately it inherited a mono – product economy – it depended on copper for over 90 percent of its foreign exchange earnings.

Zambia's debt grew from a mere $623 million in 1970 to $6.4 billion by 1987 and $7.2 billion in 1990. It had borrowed once from the IMF in 1973 – during the first oil crisis. It borrowed from this agency eleven more times after 1976. The IMF could only succeed to persuade Zambia to impose austerity conditions on Zambia in 1985 – over ten years after the first borrowing. The imposition of these measures – currency devaluation, rise in interest rates, currency auctioning, removal of subsidies, removal of price controls, freeze in wages – led to the rioting in 1986. This necessarily led to Zambia's severance of all ties to the IMF in 1987 and inevitably to most international financial institutions. It could only get back on track if it re-established the exploitative and onerous ties with the IMF.[6] It did not take Zambia long to come back to the fold of international capital. It has again embraced the IMF and the World Bank.[7] The new austerity measures required by the IMF on Zambia led to riots of June 1990, and the attempted military coup. A reconstituted Zambian political system will only succeed if it is based on a reconstituted economic system.

The grip on Zambia's economy by the World Bank, the IMF and other international financial institutions is more tight in 1991 than it was at any time in the country's history. In early 1991 for example, Zambia was ordered to clear its US$343 million arrears to the World Bank and to bring its US$1.3 billion debt to the IMF to an agreeable level within a few weeks in order to qualify for an extension of the World Bank loan in the amount of US$210 million.[8]

This is the economic context in which multi-party politics have been allowed to operate. International financial institutions and western capitalist governments are happy that this kind of politics has been permitted to operate.

The MMD supports capitalist liberalization in Zambia, therefore there is an economic and political coincidence in Zambia – the movement towards capitalist, political and economic liberalization.

It is however frightening the extent to which people in Zambia and elsewhere have accepted multi-party politics as the end-all to Zambia's political development. The analysis has ended at the point at which multi-party politics are introduced.

There is a blind eye to the historical lessons Zambia can learn from experiences of other countries. Ihonvbere as well as Falola and others have shown that in Nigeria (and other countries), multi-party politics are accompanied by corruption, embezzlement, incompetency, aggradizement, contradictions and crises, disintegration of political and economic bases and all other vices associated with dependent peripheral social formations. These developments give rise to new military coups and hence to square one.[9] Thus multipartyism should not be the end in itself, this kind of politics must ensure that corruption, mismanagement, laziness and all other negative traits that are symptoms of political and economic decay are wiped out. Political and economic accountability, limited presidential terms, judicial independence, keeping uppermost the interests of the majority of the people of Zambia and such other positive aspects must be encouraged and must replace the culture of political and economic decay. This may entail the fusion of new blood in the system. This is the continuing challenge in Zambia. However, as in the past, Zambia's political and economic trajectories will in part be determined by class as well as other struggles.

Notes

1.   See a for a good analysis of Zambia's economic crises and its interaction with international financial institutions, Roger Young and John Loxley, *Zambia: An Assessment of Zambia's structural Adjustment Experience*, (Ottawa: North-South Institute, 1990).

2.   For background, see John Mukela, "The IMF Fallout" *Africa Report*, January - February, 1989, p. 65.

3.   West Africa, (London) 11 May 1987, p. 924.

4.   Samuel Mbah, "IMF and the Third World", *National Concord* (Lagos), 9 June 1987, p. 3.

5.   Ibid.

6.   See "Zambia the slow, Malawi the poor", *The Economist*, (London) 18 February 1989, pp. 88-89.

7.   Ibid.

8.   Zambia Daily Mail, February 23, 1991, p.1.

9.   See Julius Ihonvbere, "Contradictions of Multi-Party Democracy in Peripheral Formations: The Rise and Demise of Nigeria's Second Republic 1979-1983" in Peter Meyns and Dani Wadada Nabudere (eds.) *Democracy and the One-Party-State in Africa*, (Haburg: Institut Für Afrika-Kude, 1989) pp. 257-283), Toyin Falola and Julius Ihonvbere, *The Rise and Fall of Nigeria's Second Republic, 1979-1984* (London: Zed Press, 1985).

Post-Postscript
November 1991

12

The Fall of Kenneth Kaunda, 1990 - 1991

When I wrote the major portion of this book in 1986/87, it could not be foreseen that Zambia's one-party political system would be fundamentally changed within a few years' time.[1] I had projected that the labour movement would play a significant role in the democratization of Zambia in the future, based on the role the labour movement had historically played and was currently playing in Zambia. This prognosis was not even shared by the narrow audience for which the project was initially conceived and who doubted the "provenance" of such an analysis.[2]

However, on October 31st, 1991, Kenneth Kaunda's regime was defeated in a landslide victory by the Movement for Multiparty Democracy (MMD) led by Frederick Chiluba, the Chairman-General of the Zambia Congress of Trade Unions. Kaunda had been ruling Zambia since 1964, 27 years in all. Zambia became a one-party state in 1973. As reviewed in the last two chapters, Kaunda's fall was precipitated by political events at the beginning of 1990. As also reviewed throughout this book, the events that hoisted Chiluba to the helm started germinating a long time ago from the time the labour movement gravitated towards political 'engagement' in the late seventies to the time it began to constitute itself as an unofficial opposition in the early eighties.

The events in Zambia were also overlayed by international, albeit attenuated demands for democratization in Africa as well as the changing international context triggered by events in Eastern Europe where the one-party communist systems were falling like dominoes as a result of mass protests for change.[3]

Changes in Zambia, Africa and Eastern Europe and elsewhere have taken place in the context of changing and shifting intellectual frameworks and epistemology about what kind of social forces are propelling these political changes and what are the projects-in-formation resulting from these political changes. My unit of analysis was 'class' and the process was 'class struggle' leading to a democratic space in which social democracy organized by the working class could be built.

But the debate in Africa has largely long ceased to revolve around 'class', 'class struggle', 'working class', 'dictatorship of the proletariat' etc. Over the past several years, class has been replaced by concepts of 'popular movements', 'popular classes', 'social movements' and other categories which lump people together undifferentiated by class, ideology or social belonging.

The concept of class struggle has been replaced by concepts of 'popular struggles', 'peoples struggles', 'popular alliances' and so on.[4] The end result of these struggles has been regarded as a simple democracy or multiparty democracy and human rights without any class connotation whatsoever.[5]

The shifting epistemology has not totally convinced me that the notions of 'class', 'class struggle', 'class alliance' should be abandoned. All these struggles are fundamentally aimed at serving the interests of particular segments of the populace, albeit that they may at times serve the interests of the larger society in general.[6] Even the national movements in Eastern Europe have been organized and vented by particular interests. Capitalist democracies offer ample examples that certain classes benefit more than others under capitalism and there is constant struggle for redistribution of resources.

The MMD in Zambia is a class alliance of the urbanized working class, a segment of the comprador bourgeoisie and former bureaucratic/state bourgeoisie, urban petty bourgeoisie and the lumpen proletariat. This alliance has managed to win over the rural proletariat and its populist politics ensured that it captured the interests of the entire population, given the aggrandizement of the Kaunda regime. Chiluba himself is rooted in the labour movement whose platform has always been social democracy whereby the labour movement would play its role as the protector of working class interests and divorced from state and party politics and the role of the state was to be answerable to the needs of the entire society including the working class. Because of the economic crises and increasing repression in Zambia, the working class was increasingly forced to enter the political arena as analyzed in previous chapters. Contrary to current commentary, Chiluba was never a "confirmed Marxist."[7] This would have meant that the Zambia Congress of Trade Unions which he was leading and by extension, the entire Zambian labour movement would have been informed by Marxism. As reviewed elsewhere in this book, Chiluba has always demonstrated social democratic political perspectives. Chiluba and MMD's election statements confirm his social democratic political philosophy: that he will heal Zambia by the combination of democracy, free enterprise and hard work.[8]

Kaunda's rule was based on the support of the middle class of Zambia, which class he had lavishly aggrandized for most of his rule. As indicated elsewhere, Zambia's economy was very good in the first ten years of independence and during that time, a strong middle class was allowed with state assistance to mushroom. The nationalization policy of the late sixties led to the further growth of the parastatal bourgeoisie which was beholden to Kaunda. A state bourgeoisie blossomed also without restraint.

However, from the mid-seventies onwards and particularly from the early eighties, the Zambian economy hit rock bottom and the state's failure to effectively respond to the economic crises began to increasingly alienate Kaunda's regime from its supporters. He could no longer effectively lavish the middle classes as before. The pressures of private capitalism as opposed to state capitalism further created a rapture within the alliance supporting Kaunda and his one-party state. Contrary to current analysis, Kaunda has never sponsored socialism in Zambia, instead he presided over a state capitalist system. The economic crises in Zambia were not a result of socialism but resulted from the inadequacies of dependent capitalism.

As Kaunda's hegemonic alliance became threatened by the labour movement, he increasingly became more repressive. The use of emergency powers became more widespread.[9] Despite this intimidation, the opposition to his rule became more pronounced until the critical crises of June 1990 with student riots and the attempted military coup the most serious to date. I have commented at length on that crises in the previous two chapters. The crises of 1990 severely weakened Kaunda's regime and prompted him to accept the notion of multiparty democracy.

Where does Zambia go from here? Political transformation ie multiparty politics will not necessarily lead to the solidification of democracy in Zambia. Zambia faces severe economic crisis. It is currently indebted to the tune of $9 billion[10], and this debt will keep growing for the foreseeable future. The debt crisis is as much a threat to political democracy as political autocracy itself. The debt means that the demands of the people cannot easily and immediately be met. The unmet demands will lead to frustration and eventual protests. The state may be forced to repress these demands leading to political crisis and the beginnings of the cycle of repression and violence. Political democracy can only go so far.

The heart of the above scenario is neatly captured by J. Cotler in his analysis of Peru and applies as much to Zambia and elsewhere:

> The nation's political prospects and the consolidation of democracy will depend upon the state's capacity for intermediation among sharply conflicting interests and demands in economic conditions that are hard to reconcile with popular participation by board sectors of society.[11]

The class character of the state usually emerges when crises sharply surface and the state is called upon to intermediate on behalf of a class, class fraction or a class alliance.

The solution to the resulting tenuousness of democracy painted in the above scenario is pointed out by Hutchful:

> what [is required] firstly is some formula for incorporating the popular sectors into the political process and at the economic level, responding to their basic consumption needs, thus breaking convincingly with the political and economic priorities of the former dictatorships.[12]

There is always the danger that the balance can be upset. This has to be done so carefully as not to arouse the military or to further the much feared radicalization of the political process. As has been demonstrated in Ghana, Nigeria and elsewhere, the military is always at hand to pre-empt any fundamental changes to the status quo, sometimes coming on the scene with pretensions to upset the status quo but in fact in the long run to uphold it.

The challenge for Zambia and all African countries contemplating multiparty politics remain the same:

> [can] these regimes [having] been formally redemocratised [remain] without altering any of the social, economic and political factors that unleashed undemocratic tendencies in the first place?[13]

Having emerged from the ranks of the labour movement, can the new president of Zambia serve the interests of the working class which he so vociferously demanded and espoused for so many years? He now has to consider the national constituency as a whole. Having put their man at the helm, can the Zambian labour movement continue to agitate for political and economic democracy? There are lots of challenges ahead.

Notes

1. See also Munyonzwe Hamalengwa, "The Legal System of Zambia" in Peter Sack, Carl P. Wellman and Mitsukumi Yasaki (eds.), *Monistic or Pluralistic Legal Culture? Anthropological and Ethnological Foundations of Traditional and Modern Legal Systems* (Berlin: Duncker and Humblot, 1991) pp.1-31).

2. See Munyonzwe Hamalengwa, *Thoughts are Free: Prison Experience and Reflections on Law and Politics in General* (Don Mills, Ontario: Africa in Canada Press, 1991) Chapter 21 "The Ph.D. Trap".

3. See Larry Diamond, "Ripe for Diffusion: International and Domestic Factors in the Global Trend Towards Democracy" in *Nairobi Law Monthly* (Nairobi) No. 36, September 1991, pp. 43-48.

4. A good collection of articles on these issues is, Peter Anyang' Nyong'o (ed.) *Popular Struggles for Democracy in Africa* (London and New Jersey: Zed Press and The United Nations University, 1987).

5. See various issues of *Nairobi Law Monthly* (Nairobi), For class analysis see Issa Shivji, *The Concept of Human Rights in Africa* (Dakar: Codesria, 1989). See also Munyonzwe Hamalengwa, "The Political Economy of Human Rights in Africa" *Philosophy and Social Action* (New Delhi) Vol. IX, No. 3, July-September 1983, pp. 15-26.

6. I have analyzed this issue at length in Munyonzwe Hamalengwa, "The Political Economy of Human Rights in Africa", *Ibid.*

7. Bill Schiller, "Zambian Opposition Seems Unstoppable", *Toronto Star*, October 30, 1991, p. A15.

8. *Ibid.*

9. See Munyonzwe Hamalengwa, "The Legal System of Zambia" *Supra* note 1 and *Thoughts are Free Supra* note 2.

10. Bill Schiller, "Zambian Opposition" *Supra* note 7.

11. J. Cotler, "Military Interventions and the 'Transfer of Power to Civilians' in Peru" in O'Donnell, et al; *The Transition from Authoritarian Rule: Latin America* (Baltimore: John Hopkins University Press, 1985) p. 172, Quoted in Eboe Hutchful, *infra* note 12, p. 138.

12. Eboe Hutchful, "The Debt Crisis and Its Implications for Democratization in Latin America and Africa" *Africa Development*, vol. XV, Nos. 3/4, 1990, p. 138.

13. Jorge Nef, "Redemocratisation in Latin America or Modernisation of the Status Quo" Quoted in Hutchful, *Supra* note 12.

Appendix

1. How would you categorize the nature of the relationship between the government and the labour movement in general since 1964? (Please cirle number indicating your answer)

   i very agreeable, ii agreeable, iii disagreeable, iv very disagreeable

2. Can you explain a little bit why the relationship was such as you pointed out above?

3. How would you categorize the nature of the relationship between the government and your specific union?

   i very agreeable, ii agreeable, iii disagreeable, iv very disagreeable

4. Please explain your answer here.

5. What periods (years, months in which year) do you remember as being the most agreeable or disagreeable with the government

   i most agreeable, ii most disagreeable

6. Please give reasons why you think it was so.

7. Please list workers' interests here.

8. How has the government responded to the labour movements' interests?

   i most positively responsive, ii positively responsive, iii negatively responsive, iv very negatively responsive

9. How has the government responded to your union's interests?

   i most positively responsive, ii positively responsive, iii negatively responsive, iv very negatively responsive

10. Do you think the labour movement has been effective in putting forth its interests?

    i very effective, ii effective, iii ineffective,iv very ineffective

11. Do you think your union has been effective in putting forth its interests?

    i very effective, ii effective, iii ineffective, iv very ineffective

12. Has the government the workers' interests at heart?
    i very much, ii yes, iii no, iv not at all

13. Have you heard of the Industrial Relations Act of 1971?

14. Has this Act affected in any way the labour movements' interests?
    i very much, ii yes, iii no, iv not at all

15. Please explain in what way the Act has affected the labour movement.

16. How has this Act affected your union?

17. Do you think this Act came into being to serve workers' interests?
    i very much so, ii yes, iii no, iv not at all

18. Do you think this Act came into being to serve the government's interests?
    i very much so, ii yes, iii no, iv not at all

19. Are the government's and workers' interests the same?
    i very much so, ii yes, iii no, iv not at all

20. What kind of relationship would you like to see between the government
    and the workers? Please explain.

Abbreviations

AMWU	African Mine Workers' Union
ANC	African National Congress
AFC	Agricultural Finance Company
BSA Co.	British South Africa Company
CSBZ	Cold Storage Board of Zambia
COZ	Credit Organization of Zambia
EPS	emergency powers
ZFE	Employers' Association or Zambia Federation of Employees
FINDECO	Financial Development Corporation
FNDP	First National Development Plan
IPD	Industrial Participatory Democracy
IRA	Industrial Relations Act
IRC	Industrial Relations Court
ICFTU	International Confederation of Free Trade Unions
MUZ	Mineworkers Union of Zambia
MINDECO	Mining Development Corporation
MMD	Movement for Multi-party Democracy
NAMBOARD	National Agricultural Marketing Board
NUBEGW	National Union of Building, Engineering and General Workers
NUCIW	National Union of Commercial and Industrial Workers
NUPSW	National Union of Public Services Workers

NCCM	Nchanga Consolidated Copper Mines
NRARWTU	Northern Rhodesia African Railway Workers Trade Union
RWUZ	Railway Workers Union of Zambia
RTUC	Reformed Trade Union Congress
RDC	Rural Development Corporation
SNDP	Second National Development Plan
TAZARA	Tanzania and Zambia Railway
TFL	Tanzania Federation of Labour
TBZ	Tobacco Board of Zambia
TUC	Trade Union Congress
UNIP	United National Independence Party
UPP	United Progressive Party
UTUC	United Trade Union Congress
WCs	Works Councils
ZCTU	Zambia Congress of Trade Unions
ZFE	Zambia Federation of Employers
ZIMCO	Zambia Industrial and Mining Corporation
ZNUT	Zambia National Union of Teachers

Select Bibliography

PRIMARY SOURCES

1. Official Publications and Documents

Kaunda, K.D.

Zambia Shall be Free: An Autobiography. London: Heinemann Educational Books Ltd., 1962.

Humanism in Zambia and a Guide to its Implementation Part I. Lusaka: Zambia Information Service, 1967.

'Zambia's Economic Revolution'. An Address to the National Council of UNIP at Mulungushi (19th April). Lusaka: Zambia Information Service, 1968a.

'Zambia's Guideline for the Next Decade'. An Address to the National Council of UNIP at Mulungushi (9th November). Lusaka: Zambia Information Service, 1968b.

'Towards Complete Independence'. An address to the National Council of UNIP at Matero Hall, (11th August). Lusaka: Zambia Information Service, 1969.

'Take Up the Challenge'. An Address to the National Council of UNIP, Mulungushi Hall, (7th-10th November). Lusaka: Zambia Information Service, 1970.

'A Path For The Future'. An Address to UNIP Sixth General Conference, Mulungushi Hall (8th May). Lusaka: Zambia Information Service, 1971.

'You Hold the Key to the Success of Participatory Democracy'. Lusaka: Zambia Information Service, 1972a.

'A Nation of Equals' - The Kabwe Declaration Addresses to the National Council of UNIP Hindu Hall, Kabwe (1st-3rd December), 1972b.

Humanism in Zambia and a Guide to Its Implementation Part II. Lusaka: Government Printer, 1974.

'The Watershed'. An Address to the National Council of UNIP Mulungushi Hall, Lusaka (June 30-July 3) (mineo.), 1975a.

'Education for Revolution'. Lusaka: Zambia Information Service: Background No.36/75, 1975b.

A Humanist in Africa. Letters to Collin M. Morris from Kenneth D. Kaunda, President of Zambia. London and Lusaka Veritas, 1976.

Humanism in Zambia and a Guide to Its Implementation (Lusaka: Kenneth Kaunda Foundation, 1987).

Politics in Zambia, Vol. 1, (Lusaka: Kenneth Kaunda Foundation, 1988).

Republic of Zambia

Constitution of Zambia: Appendix I to the Laws of Zambia, Vol.XVI. Lusaka: Government Printer, 1965.

First National Development Plan 1966-1970. Lusaka: Office of National Development and Planning, 1966.

Second National Development Plan 1972-1976. Lusaka: Ministry of Development Planning and National Guidance, 1971a.

Supplement to the Republic of Zambia Government Gazette, October 19, No.30 of 1971, 1971b.

Village Productivity and Ward Development Committee - A Pocket Manual. Lusaka. Government Printer, 1971c.

The Industrial Relations Act, 1971; No.36 of 1971. Lusaka: Government Printer, 1971d.

Reports of the Working Party Appointed to Review the System of Decentralised Administration. Lusaka: Cabinet Office (May), 1972a.

Report of the National Commission on the Establishment of a One-Party Participatory Democracy in Zambia: Summary of Recommendations Accepted By Government (Government Paper No.1 of 1972). Lusaka: Government Printer, 1972b.

Report of the National Commission On the Establishment of a One-Party Participatory Democracy in Zambia. Lusaka: Government Printer (October), 1972c.

Report of the Working Party Appointed to Review the System of Decentralised Administration (Simmance Report). Lusaka: Cabinet Office, 1972d.

Supplement to the Republic of Zambia Government Gazette dated 25th August, 1973: *The Constitution of Zambia Act (No.27 of 1973)*. Lusaka: Government Printer, 1973.

Report of the Commission of Inquiry into the Salaries, Salary Structure and Conditions of Service, Vol.1, The Public Services and the Parastatal Sector, 1975.

Economic Reports. Lusaka: Ministry of Development Planning, 1976-1984.

Third National Development Plant, 1979-1983. Lusaka: Ministry of Development Planning and Office of the President, 1979.

Ministry of Finance

Annual Economic Reports, 1971-1984.

Ministry of Labour and Social Services

Annual Economic Reports, 1976-1983.

2. Oral and Written Evidence

Anonymous: Dozens of Government and Private Individuals. Lusaka and Kitwe, 1985 and 1988.

Chilomo, Phillip, Zambia Cooperative Federation, Lusaka. Ongoing.

Chitala, Derrick, Small Industrial Development Organisation, Lusaka. Ongoing since August 1985.

Glover, Thomas, Bureau of Mines, Washington, D.C., January 25, 1983.

Gran, Guy, Development Consultant, Washington, D.C.,February-March 1983.

Hanlon, Joe, Journalist, London. March 4, 1987. Toronto.

Himwiinga, Paulsen, Kenneth Kaunda Foundation, Lusaka. Ongoing.

Ikowa, L.B., National Chairman, National Union of Plantation and Agricultural Workers, March 16, 1987. (Questionnaire)

Kaiko Muvoywa M., Zambia National Union of Teachers, Lusaka. March 16, 1987. (Questionnaire)

Kasumbu Ignatius M., National Union of Commercial and Industrial Workers. March 16, 1987. (Questionnaire)

King, Philip, Country Officer for Zambia, Department of State, Washington, D.C. January 1983.

Low Ambassador, Former U.S. Ambassador to Zambia, Washington, D.C. February 1983.

Momba, Jotham, Lecturer, University of Zambia. Lusaka. Ongoing.

Mubanga, J., Railway Workers Union of Zambia, March 13, 1987. (Questionnaire)

Ngonda, Ambassador, Zambian Ambassador to the U.S.A., Washington, D.C. February 1983.

O'Brien, Michael F., U.S. Information Agency, Africa Section, Washington, D.C., March 1983.

Savastak, David, U.S. Department of Commerce, Washington, D.C. February 18, 1983.

Simatendele, N. L., Zambia National Union of Teachers. March 16, 1987. (Questionnaire)

Silwimba, S.I., General Secretary, National Union of Plantation and Agricultural Workers, March 16, 1987. (Questionnaire)

Simuchoba Sibanze, Advocate of the High Court of Zambia. Ongoing.

Sumani, M.K., Mineworkers Union of Zambia, March 11, 1987. (Questionnaire)

Walamba, Timothy, Chairman, Mineworkers Union of Zambia, March 11, 1987. (Questionnaire)

Wilkoski Ambassador, Former U.S. Ambassador to Zambia, Washington, D.C., February 1983.

3. Newspapers

Times of Zambia
Zambia Daily Mail
National Mirror
The Workers Voice

SECONDARY SOURCES

1. Books

Ake, Claude. *Revolutionary Pressures in Africa*. (London: Zed Press, 1978.)

Allen, V.L., *Trade Union Leadership*. (Cambridge, Mass.: Harvard University Press, 1957.)

Ananaba, W. *The Trade Union Movement in Nigeria*. (London: Hurst, 1969.)

Arrighi, G. and Saul, J. *Essays on the Political Economy of Africa*. (New York: Monthly Review Press, 1973.)

Bates, R. *Union, Parties and Political Development in Zambia*. (New Haven and London: Yale University Press, 1971.)

Baylies, C. *The State and Class Formation in Zambia*, PH.D. dissertation, University of Wisconsin, Madison, 1978.

Berger, E. *Labour, Race and Colonial Rule*. (London: OUP, 1974).

Bettelheim, Charles, *Class Struggles in the USSR*, 2 Volumes. (New York and London: Monthly Review Press, 1976 and 1978).

Braverman, H. *Labour and Monopoly Capital: The Degradation of Work in the Twentieth Century*. (New York: Monthly Review Press, 1974).

Burawoy, M. *The Colour of Class on the Copper Mines*, (Lusaka: UNZA, Institute for African Studies, 1972).

Cohen, Robin (ed). *Forced Labour in Colonial Africa*. (London: Zed Press, 1979).

_____. *Labour and Politics in Nigeria*. (London: Heinemann, 1974).

Crisp, Jeff, *The Story of An African Working Class*, (London: Zed Press, 1984.)

Daniel, P. *Africanization, Nationalization and Inequality*, (Cambridge: CUP, 1979).

Draisma, Tom, *The Struggle Against Underdevelopment in Zambia since Independence: What Role for Education* (Amsterdam: Free University Press, 1987).

Dunlop, J. *Industrial Relations System*. (New York: (Henry Holt and Co., 1958).

Evans, P. *Dependent Development: The Alliance of Multinationals, State and Local Capital in Brazil*. (Princeton: Princeton University Press, 1979).

Eyoh, Dickson. *State, Capital and Agrarian Transformation in Nigeria: Politics and Production in Lafia, Plateau State* (Ph.D. Thesis, York University, 1989).

Falola, T. and Julius Ihonvbere, *The Rise and Fall of Nigeria's Second Republic* (London: Zed Press, 1985).

Fann, K.T. and Donald C. Hodges (eds). *Readings in U.S. Imperialism*. (Boston: Porter Sargent, 1971).

Fanon, Frantz. 1967. *The Wretched of the Earth*. (London: Penguin).

Freeman, *The Politics of Mixed Economies* (Ithaca: Cornell University Press, forthcoming)

Freud, Bill. *Capital and Labour in the Nigerian Tin Mines*. (London: Longman, 1980).

Fransman, M. (ed). *Industry and Accumulation in Africa*. (London: Heinemann, 1982).

Fry, J. *Employment and Income Distribution in the African Economy*. (London: Croom Helm, 1979).

Gramsci, A. *Prison Notebooks*. (New York: International Publishers, 1980).

Gutkind, P.C.W., Cohen R. and Copans, J. (eds). *African Labour History*. (London: Sage, 1979).

_____ and I. Wallerstein, (eds). *The Political Economy of Contemporary Africa*, (Beverly Hills: Sage, 1976).

_____ and Waterman, P. (eds.) *African Social Studies: A Radical Reader*. (New York: Monthly Review Press, 1977).

Hamalengwa, Munyonzwe, *Thoughts are Free: Prison Experience and Reflections on Law and Politics in General* (Toronto: Africa in Canada Press, 1991).

Hyman, R. *Marxism and the Sociology of Trade Unionism*. (London: Plute Press, 1971).

_____. *Strikes*. (London: Fontana, 1972).

_____. *Industrial Relations: A Marxist Introduction*. (London: Macmillan, 1975).

Ihonvbere, Julius, *Labour, Transnational Corporations and the State in Nigeria's Oil Industry* (Ph.D. Thesis, University of Toronto, 1984).

Jeffries, R., *Class, Power and Ideology in Ghana: The Railwaymen of Secondi*. (Cambridge, 1970).

Kalula, E. Ed. *Some Aspects of Zambian Labour Relations*. (Lusaka: National Archives of Zambia, 1975).

Katz Stephen, *Marxism, Africa and Social Class: A Critique of Relevant Theories*. (Montreal: McGill University Centre for Developing-Area Studies, 1980).

Kasoma Francis, *The Press in Zambia* (Lusaka: Multimedia, 1986)

Laclau, Ernesto, *Politics and Ideology in Marxist Theory*. (London: New Left Books, 1977).

Lapides, Kenneth., *Marx and Engels on the Trade Unions* (New York: Praeger, 1987).

Lenin, V.I., *The Development of Capitalism in Russia*. (Moscow: Progress Publishers, 1956).

_____. *Collected Works*, 45 Volumes.

Leys, Colin, *Underdevelopment in Kenya*. (London: Heinemann Books, 1975).

Marx, K. *Capital*, 3 Volumes.

_____and Engels, F. *Selected Works*, 3 Volumes.

Meebelo, Henry, S., *African Proletarians and Colonial Capitalism* (Lusaka: Kenneth Kaunda Foundation, 1986).

_____,*Reaction to Colonialism* (Manchester: Manchester University Press, 1971).

Meynaud J. and A. Salah Bey. *Trade Unionism in Africa.* (London. 1967).

Meyns, P. and Dani Wadada Nabudere, (eds.), *Democracy and the One-Party State in Africa* (Hamburg: Institut Fr Afrika-Kunde, 1989).

Mijere Nsolo, *The Mineworkers' Resistance to Governmental Decentralization in Zambia* (Ph.D. Thesis, Brandeis, 1985).

Moore, David, *The Contradictory Construction of Hegemony in Zimbabwe: Politics, Ideology, and Class in the Formation of a New African State* (PH.D. Thesis, York University, Toronto, 1990.)

Mulford, D. Zambia: *The Politics of Independence.* (Oxford. 1967).

Mwaanga, Vernon J., *The Other Society: A Detainee's Diary* (Lusaka: Fleetfoot, 1987).

Ndulo M. and K. Turner. *Civil Liberties Cases in Zambia.* (Oxford. 1984).

Nwabueze, B. *Presidentialism in Commonwealth Africa.* (London. Hurst, 1974).

Ollawa, P. *Participatory Democracy in Zambia.* (Devon: Ilfracombe, 1979).

Osei-Hwedie K. and Muna Ndulo (eds.) *Issues in Zambian Development* (Nyangwe and Roxbury: Omenana, 1985).

Parpart, J. *Labour and Capital on the African Copperbelt*, (Philadelphia: Temple University Press, 1983).

Peace, Adrian. *Class, Choice and Conflict in Nigeria.* (Hassocks: Harvester Books, 1979).

Perrings, C. *Black Mineworkers in Central Africa.* (New York, 1979).

Poulantzas, Nicos, *Political Power and Social Classes.* Translated by Timothy O'Hagan. (London: New Left Books, 1973).

_____. *Fascism and Dictatorship: The Third International and the Problem of Fascism.* (London: New Left Books, 1974).

_____. *Classes in Contemporary Capitalism.* Translated by David Fernbach. (London: New Left Books, 1975).

Sandbrook, Richard. *Proletarians and African Capitalism. The Kenyan Case 1962-70.* (Cambridge: Cambridge University Press, 1975).

_____. *The Politics of Basic Needs.* (Toronto: University of Toronto Press, 1982).

and R. Cohen (eds). *The Development of an African Working Class.* (London: Longmans, 1975).

Saul, John, *The State and Revolution in Eastern Africa.* (New York and London: Monthly Review Press, 1979).

Shivji, Issa. *Class Struggles in Tanzania.* (New York: Monthly Review, 1976).

_____. *Law, State and The Working Class in Tanzania.* (London: James Currey, 1986).

Sklar, Richard, *Corporate Power in An African State.* (Berkeley: University of California Press, 1975).

Szeftel, M. *Conflict, Spoils and Class Formation in Zambia*, PH.D Dissertation, University of Manchester, 1978.

Therborn, Goran. *What Does the Ruling Class Do When it Rules?* (London: New Left Books/Verso, 1978).

_____. *Science, Class and Society.* (London: New Left Books/Verso, 1980).

Thomas, C. *The Rise of the Authoritarian State in Peripheral Societies.* (New York: Monthly Review Press, 1984).

Thompson, E. P., *The Making of the English Working Class.* (Harmondsworth: Penguin, 1963).

_____. *Whigs and Hunters.* (New York: Pantheon, 1975).

Tordoff, W. Ed. *Politics in Zambia.* (Berkeley: University of California Press, 1974).

_____. Ed. *Administration in Zambia.* (Manchester: University of Manchester Press, 1980).

Trotsky, L. *Marxism and the Trade Unions.* (London: New Park Publications, 1972).

Turok, Ben. ed. *Development in Zambia.* (London: Zed Press, 1981).

Van Onselen, C. *Chibaro: African Mine Labour in Southern Rhodesia 1900-1933.* (London: Pluto Press, 1976).

Woldring, Klaas and C. Chibwe, eds., *Beyond PoliticalIndependence: Zambia's Development Predicament in the 1980s* (Berlin et al.: Mouton, 1984).

Young, R. and John Loxley, *Zambia: An Assessment of Zambia's Structural Adjustment Experience,* (Ottawa: North-South Institute, 1990).

2. Articles

Alavi, Hamza. "The State in Post-Colonial Societies: Pakistan and Bangladesh", *New Left Review* 74 (July-August, 1972).

Baylies C. and M. Szeftel, "The Rise of a Zambian Capitalist Class in the 1970s" *Journal of Southern African Studies* Vol. 8, No. 2, 1982.

Beckman, B. 'State Capitalism and Public Enterprise in Africa', in Ghai, Y. (ed.), *Law in the Political Economy of Public Enterprise: African Perspectives.* (Uppsala: Scandinavian Institute of African Studies, 1977).

_____. "Imperialism and the National Bourgeoisie" *Review of African Political Economy* 22 (1981).

_____. "Whose State: State and Capitalist Development in Nigeria". *Review of African Political Economy* 23 (1982).

Berberoglu, Berch, "The Nature and Contradictions of State Capitalism in the Third World", *Social and Economic Studies* 28 (2), (June, 1979).

Brenner, Robert. "The Origins of Capitalist Development: A Critique of Neo-Smithian Marxism", *New Left Review,* No.104, (1977).

Cohen, R. "Nigeria's Labour Leader NO. 1: Notes for a Biographical Study of M.A.O. Imoudu", *Journal of the Historical Society of Nigeria*, Vol.5, No.2, (1970).

_____. "From Peasants to Workers in Africa", in P. Gutkind, and I. Wallerstein, (eds), *The Political Economy of Contemporary Africa*. (London: Sage, 1976).

_____. "Michael Imoudu and the Nigeria Labour Movement", *Race and Class*, Vol.3, (Spring, 1977).

_____. "Resistance and Hidden Forms of Consciousness Amongst African Workers", *Review of African Political Economy*, No.19, (1980).

and David Michael. "The Revolutionary Potential of the African Lumpenproletariat: A Sceptical View" *Institute of Development Studies Bulletin*, Vol.5, No.2-3, (1973).

Cox, Robert. "Approaches to the Futurology of Industrial Relations", *International Institute of Labour Studies Bulletin*, No.8, (1971).

_____. "Labour and Hegemony", *International Organization*, Vol.31, No.3, (1977).

Cross, S. "Politics and Criticism in Zambia" *Journal of Southern African Studies*, 1,1, (1974).

Fincham, R. and Grace Zulu, "Labour and Participation in Zambia" in *Development in Zambia*. Ed. B. Turok, (London: Zed, 1981).

Freyhold, Michela Von. "The Post-Colonial State and its Tanzanian Version", *Review of African Political Economy* 8 (January-April, 1977).

Gertzel, C. "Labour and State: The Case of Zambia's Mineworkers Union" *Journal of Commonwealth and Comparative Politics*, 13,3, (1975).

_____. "Industrial Relations in Zambia to 1975" in *Industrial Relations in Africa*. Ed. Ukandi Damachi et al. (New York: Macmillan, (1979).

Gold, David; Clarence Lo, and Erik Olin Wright. "Recent Developments in Marxist Theories of the Capitalist State", *Monthly Review* (7) (October, 1975) and (November, 1975).

Gouldborne, Harry. "The Problem of the State in Backward Capitalist Societies", *African Development* VI, (1), (1981).

Hamalengwa, Munyonzwe, "The Political Economy of Human Rights in Africa", *Philosophy and Social Action* Vol. IX, No. 3,(July-September, 1983) pp 15-26.

_____. "The Legal System of Zambia" in Peter Sack, Carl Wellman and Mitsukuni Yasaki, (eds). *Monistic or Pluralistic Legal Culture? Anthropological and Ethnological Foundations of Traditional and Modern Legal Systems*. (Berlin: Duncker & Humblot, 1991) pp 1-31.

Henderson, Ian. "Workers and the State in Colonial Zambia" in *Evolving Structure of Zambian Society* (Centre of African Studies, Edinburg, 1980).

Hoogvelt, Ankie, "Indigenization and Technological Dependency", *Development and Change 11* (2), (April, 1980).

Hopkins, A.G. "The Lagos Strike of 1897: An Exploration in Nigerian Labour History". *Past and Present* 35 (December, 1966).

Hyman, R. "Third World Strikes in International Perspective", *Development and Change*, Vol.10, (2), (1979).

Leys, Colin, "The Over-developed Post-Colonial State: A Re-Evaluation", *Review of African Political Economy* 5 (January-April, 1976).

Mudenda, G. "Class Formation and Class Struggle in Contemporary Zambia" in *Proletarianization and Class Struggle in Africa*, ed. by Magubane, B. and Nzongola-Ntalaja, (San Francisco: Synthesis Publications, 1983).

Mueller Susanne, "The Historical Origins of Tanzania's Ruling Class" *Canadian Journal of African Studies* Vol. 15, No. 3, 1981.

Ollman, Bertell, "Studying Class Consciousness" *The Insurgent Sociologist* Vol.14, No. 1, 1987.

Parpart, J. and Shaw, T., "Contradictions and Coalition: Class Fractions in Zambia, 1964 to 1984" in *Africa Today*. 30, 3, (1983).

Sandbrook, Richard. "The State and the Development of Trade Unionism" in G. Hyden, R. Jackson and J. Okumu (eds). *Development Administration*. (London: Oxford University Press, 1970).

_____. "Patrons, Clients and Unions: The Labour Movement and Political Conflict in Kenya" *Journal of Commonwealth Studies* 16 (1972).

_____. "The Working Class in the Future of the Third World". *World Politics* 15 (3), (1973).

_____. "The Political Potential of African Urban Workers", *Canadian Journal of African Studies* Vol.XI (3), (1979).

_____. "Worker Consciousness and Popular Protest in Tropical Africa" in R.L. and I.H.

Simpson (eds). *Research in the Sociology of Work*. (Greenwich: JAI Press, 1981).

Saul, John S. "The State in Post-Colonial Societies: Tanzania" *Socialist Register* (1974).

Scarritt, J. "The Analysis of Social Class, Political Participation and Public Policy in Zambia" *Africa Today*, 30, 3, (1983).

Shaw, T. "The Political Economy of Zambia" *Current History*. (March 1982).

_____. "Zambia After Twenty Years: Recession and Repression Without Revolution" *Issue*, XII, 1/2, (1982).

Sichone, Owen B., "One-Party Participatory Democracy and Socialist Orientation: The De-Politicization of the Masses in Post-Colonial Zambia" in Peter Meyns and Dani Wadada Nabudere (eds.) *Democracy and the One-Party-State in Africa* (Hamburg: Institut Fr Afrika-Kunde, 1989).

Southall, T. "Zambia: Class Formation and Government Policies in the 1970s" *Journal of Southern African Studies*, 7, 1, (1980).

Szeftel, M. "The Political Process in Post-Colonial Zambia: The Factional Bases of Factional Conflict" in *The Evolving Structure of Zambian Society*, (Centre of African Studies, Edinburg, 1980).

Waterman, Peter. "The 'Labour Aristocracy' in Africa: Introduction to a Debate", *Development and Change*, Vol.6, (3), (1975).

_____. "Conservatism Amongst Nigerian Workers", in Williams, G. (ed). *Nigeria: Economy and Society*. London: Collins, 1976.

_____. "African Workers and African Capitalism", (Book Review), *British Journal of Industrial Relations*, Vol.14, (2), (1977).

Woldring, K. "Corruption and Inefficiency in Zambia: Recent Inquiries and Their Results" *Africa Today*. 30, 3, (1983).

Index

About the Author

Munyonzwe Hamalengwa is a lawyer who practices Criminal Law and Immigration Law in Toronto, Canada. He is from Zambia. He has studied at the Universities of Zambia, Carleton and York (Toronto). He has published in the areas of international human rights law and economic and political development in the developing world. He has also written a political and legal autobiography *Thoughts Are Free: Prison Experience and Reflections On Law and Politics in General* (Don Mills, Ontario: Africa in Canada Press, 1991).